MISSED THE MEMO

THE TOP 9 THINGS I WISH I WOULD HAVE KNOWN ABOUT COLLEGE FROM THE START

Aurora Alexander

MISSED THE MEMO :

The Top 9 Things I Wish I Would Have Known About College From The Start

Copyright © 2019 by Aurora Alexander.

Cover art by Rob Williams, Cover Designer, Fiverr.com/cal5086
Photography by Melinda Miller, MK Miller Photography

For information contact :
http://www.auroraalexander.com

ISBN: 9781733602570
First Edition: February 2019

CONTENTS

Memo #1

It's Not Like the Movies

"All fantasy should have a solid base in reality." –
Max Beerbohm.

When I was a little girl, I wanted to be a mermaid. I loved everything about the water. I loved the animals. I loved swimming. I was obsessed with Disney's *The Little Mermaid*.[1] My mom told me she named me after the main character of that story, but it was not the Disney version. In this story, instead of the lead character "Ariel" as a mermaid princess, her name was "Aurora." It was serendipity. (Looking back now, she may have just been humoring me.) I knew I was destined to be a mermaid. I knew I would spend the rest of my days living it up in the ocean. I could see it all in the theatre of my mind.

Imagine how crushed I was to realize that I would, in fact, NEVER become a mermaid. To be frank, I was a lot older than anyone would care to admit. I was around 7 or 8-years-old. *Don't judge!* Not to get into a bunch of detail, but I remember right where I was standing when the realization hit me like a ton of bricks. I needed to quickly change my answer to the dreaded question that so many adults ask children, "What do you want to be when you grow up?"

I remember asking my mom what I could do for a job that would allow me to swim with dolphins and marine life all day. She told me that perhaps I could be a marine biologist. This was an interesting concept. I wasn't sure what a marine biologist did, but I could imagine. I watched reruns of *The Undersea World of Jacques Cousteau*[2] from time to time and was always intrigued. Would this now be my new dream and my new answer to the what-do-you-want-to-be question? After consulting my Magic 8 Ball, all signs pointed to "Yes!"

As luck would have it, this is also around the same time I visited Sea World for the first time, which was a chain of theme parks that featured aquariums and marine life galore. I was in awe of all the marine life and the lucky individuals who got to work with these great beasts.

What a job! These people actually get paid to swim and play all day!

I couldn't believe my eyes. I remember conjuring up enough courage to talk with one of the animal trainers between shows to ask them some questions about the job. I asked one woman what degree she got in college. She said she majored in marine biology. *YES! Marine Biology! She is a marine biologist!* This affirmation just solidified my new career field of choice. I would be a marine biologist and work at Sea World someday. I would have all the fun of a mermaid, but still keep my legs. *Bonus!*

For the next 10 years, I was on track to become a marine biologist. I looked at colleges for their marine biology/marine science programs. I knew I would have to move for school and work. So, I had slowly but surely been preparing myself, and my family, for my inevitable departure. I even got a job at Sea World as an Ama Diver (pearl diver) hoping to get my foot in the door. Although my job comprised of working with oysters, which are the most docile of all the sea creatures, I was still working within the field. I also used my job as an opportunity to rub elbows with the animal trainers that were working with the dolphins and other marine life at the park.

I had finally decided to attend a university that is located near Myrtle Beach, SC because I had family in the area and I knew some animal trainers had gone to school there. I was confident going into this new leg of my adventure. I remember talking with one of my animal trainer friends and asking her for some last-minute advice before I left for school. I wanted to squeeze as much information out so I would be totally prepared for this new chapter. Unfortunately, the information I got from her concerned me.

She told me, "Whatever you do, do NOT tell them you work at Sea World or that you want to play with dolphins." *You're kidding, right?* Nope, she wasn't kidding. She told me how that profession was viewed by the faculty within the marine science department and that it would be best to leave out that chapter of my life when discussing my long-term career goals. I walked away from that exchange more than a little confused. I was concerned about my future.

Fast forward to my first day of classes at my new university. I'm sitting in my Marine Biology course, and my instructor asks the class a question. "Who in here would like to work with Sea World someday?" *Here it is. She warned me about this.* I kept my hand down because the former student had already cautioned me. Unfortunately, other people in my class may have missed that memo. Out of a class of around 40 students, over half of them raised their hands. You should have seen the scowl on the instructor's face. *He set them up!* At that point, he berated the students for their choice of occupation/employer. You also have to take into consideration that this was before the era of the *Black Fish*[3] documentary and the controversy that surrounded captive killer whales. Thanks to the movie, the public was made aware of some unsavory practices this mega theme park performed. This was 20 years ago though. Society is more cognizant of sensitive issues like that now than they were back then.

It is probably no surprise I ended up leaving that university early on and coming back home. Considering the courses I was taking and how they didn't really align with my needs/wants, I didn't see the point. Here I was doing topography assignments, mapping the ocean floor, but all I wanted to do was play with dolphins. The marine biologist route seemed to be way off course from my real desires. So,

I came back home and switched gears.

• • •

Want to know how many times I officially changed my major in school after that? Over ten times. For those of you finding it hard to recognize that number that is a one (1) with a zero behind it (0). *That's double digits, folks.* Since my whole childhood and early adulthood consisted of dreams of being a marine biologist, I didn't know how to pick a major or focus on a career field.

The Student Research Foundation did a study where they tried to find the factors motivating a high school student's choice of potential majors/career fields.[4] This study concluded that 71% of students picked based on their interests. My interests were dolphins and marine life. I didn't see a lot of dolphins and marine life in a land-locked state like West Virginia. I don't remember encountering any orcas or lion seals as I hiked through the hills of Appalachia. *So... veto! Next.* The study also showed that a considerable amount of students chose an occupation based on their parents. Well, my dad was a coal miner. My dad's dad and my mom's dad were coal miners. All of my uncles were coal miners. I would not be a coal miner. I have nothing against the profession at all. I know that coal miners put their lives on the line every single day, but I didn't see that in my future. *Veto! Next.* My mom? My mom was a nurse and hated it. She always worked evenings and weekends. She was also never around on my birthday or holidays because of her job. Nursing is a 24/7 job. I didn't want that for myself, and my mom didn't want that for me either. *Veto! Next.*

My major exploration methods throughout college

caused a journey that was riddled with mistakes and missteps. This ultimately led to countless failed and dropped classes, not to mention a hiatus or four from college. *Who's counting?* The confusion about my next steps made my path towards graduation seem virtually impossible. To say my direction in school was unclear would be the understatement of the decade. Unfortunately, for the longest time, even after I graduated with my master's degree, I believed I was the ONLY one who bumbled their way through college. Little did I know, I am not the only student to ever meander around the puzzling path towards graduation.

• • •

Flash forward to today, I work as an academic advisor at a university. Every summer I work new student orientation. I meet with incoming freshman to discuss courses for the fall semester. This also gives me the opportunity to learn more about the student, and the path they want to take that will lead them to their desired career. Most incoming freshmen are bright-eyed and bushy-tailed, excited about the new adventure that lies ahead. I always ask a student why they chose their specific major. I work in the Department of Psychological Sciences, so, most students will answer with "I just want to help people." Then when I ask about what kind of job or career they see themselves in, I get a lot of answers that pertain to something they've seen on TV or in the movies.

Claire was the perfect example of this typical student. I asked Claire what she would like to do after she graduated from college. She said she would like to one day become a criminal profiler because her favorite show was *Criminal*

Minds.[5] She also mentioned that she was interested in a possible double major in criminal studies. I asked her what made her interested in that subject. She said one day she would like to go to law school. As I inquired more, I asked her about her interest in law. Claire said she was interested in law because her favorite movie was *Legally Blond*.[6] She said she could really see herself in a courtroom trying a case. This gave me great concern as an advisor because the student was deciding based on expectations set by Hollywood. In talking with Claire, I could see that she was not making an informed decision about her future. Claire reminded me of me when I was an incoming freshman.

On the flip side, I met with Michael who wanted to come in to talk about possibly changing his major from psychology. He was also considering a minor in criminology. Michael said he originally started in psychology because he wanted to be a forensic psychologist. I asked him how he came to know the profession. With a roll of his eyes and a heavy sigh, he said that he loved *Law and Order: SVU* and *CSI*.[7] However, he said he did actual research on what a forensic psychologist does and it wasn't nearly as interesting or as glamorous as he was expecting. He was now questioning his original career goal and seeking more information about alternatives that would align with his wants and needs.

The key element to these students' stories is the research component. I did my own research when I was trying to find out what a marine biologist does, but it was surface level investigating. I didn't do a deep dive (pun intended) into the career field until after I took courses. Sometimes you will not know until you take courses within a major before you realize that it's not what you thought it would be. It might take a conversation or two with individuals that work in the field for you to glean concrete information about your potential career choice through informational interviews. (I will speak in more detail about informational interviews in Memo #5: Networking.) Whatever it is, you should be absorbing a ton of relevant information from different sources so you are making well-informed decisions about your educational journey that align with your career goals.

• • •

What is the "average" college experience?

Answers vary depending on the person and their background, which may include socio-economic status, age, race, gender, culture and even portrayals of college life in today's media. These factors shape and mold the potential student's expectations of what their college experience *should* look like or *ought* to be. However, everyone's college experience has the potential of looking very different from what was originally expected. When expectations collide with reality, the results may not initially be positive, but there is always the possibility of growth and development.

Most of my expectations of college had a lot to do with how college life was portrayed on television and movies. College life seemed filled with friends and parties. It seemed more social than educational, which sounded exciting to a high school student. The only time I ever saw one of these characters study was if that character was portrayed as a "nerd" or if someone had an impending exam. A character would usually prepare for these exams using an overnight cram session, depicted by a musical montage. In the theatre of my mind, I can just see the montage now.

Fun music... a library at night... Stacks of opened books... wads of crinkled papers litter the table tops and floor... pencil behind the ear... blood-shot eyes... a friend falls asleep while reading a textbook with mouth agape as drool trickles out... student suddenly jerks awake and calls it a night... barely makes it to class in slippers and pajamas... aces the exam and gives the professor a wink while strolling out the door.

Everything always seemed to work itself out. It seemed easy and manageable.

These portrayals were reinforced by the realities of my high school experience. I never really had to study because high school came easily. I was a good student and was in all the honors classes. I made straight A's, and I was in the National Honor Society. Sometimes I encountered a difficult paper or an important test, but good grades were usually achieved by staying up the night before to prepare. I really didn't have to try in high school, and I assumed that my college experience would be very similar. I expected it to be a little more difficult, but I was sure I would acclimate to the transition just as easily as I did from elementary school to middle school and from middle school to high school.

My first year of college differed from the traditional college student. I was a senior in high school, but I was eligible for a program called "post-secondary education." Instead of going to high school, I took college classes my senior year. Some classes were easy for me. I still had to try because I had to produce homework and papers, but again, the good grades seemed almost effortless. However, I encountered a class that no matter what I did, I could not understand the concepts and I always failed the test.

I had never been in a situation like this before. I went to every class, and I read the chapters. When the test came, I failed it. I went over the notes, and I even met with a tutor, but I still failed the exams.

I had never felt so defeated in all of my life. The television shows and movies never portrayed a character who did everything in their power to succeed in college and still failed. The overnight cram sessions didn't seem to work. I was completely stumped how to even study for this subject. I used everything in my student arsenal, but nothing seemed to work. I was also struggling with my motivation to do well because I had no focus. My path to my dream job was destroyed because I no longer needed to be a marine biologist. I was circling the drain in college. I felt like college was happening *to* me instead of me being an active participant.

My grades for the first semester of college were less than stellar. I ended up with an A, B, C and F. Failing a class completely deflated my confidence while annihilating all of my expectations of what my college experience *should* be. My performance in the following semesters steadily declined to where I was receiving all D's and F's. The student who never had to try to succeed suddenly found herself in a position that seemed she couldn't succeed no matter how hard she tried. I felt like a failure, which gave me no desire to continue my educational endeavors. I was convinced that

I wasn't meant for college.

My reality of college led to a rude awakening of just how difficult life could be, which differed vastly from the glossy portrayals of college life I expected from the media. I took a hiatus from college because I thought I could make it on my own. I knew of people that had achieved success in life without a college degree, and I was convinced that I would take the same path. As the years passed, I continued to try to make something of myself without a college education, but I was getting nowhere fast. I realized that I needed a college education to succeed in life, but I was bitter and confused about my experience.

I doubted myself, wondering if I had what it took to be successful in college. I was scared that I wasn't smart enough to absorb the material I was learning to achieve good grades. I was insecure about my previous performance, but I knew the path I was on would not lead me to where I wanted to go in life. After years of bitterness, I swallowed my pride and consulted with an academic advisor about coming back to school.

I knew I needed to refocus on learning the material rather than becoming consumed with the grade and whether or not the course was directly related to my future dream job. I realized that if I fully understood the concepts I was learning, then the grades would reflect my understanding. I had to re-frame my perception and focus on what was most important. The grade, just like the degree, was just a reflection of how well I understood the education. I wanted to *earn* the grade which would eventually allow me to *earn* my degree. My goal had shifted to concentrating on the process of learning rather than focusing merely on the outcome.

Years later, my expectations of college differed greatly from when I originally started. I realized that college wasn't *difficult*, but it was *demanding*. Being a successful student required me to take my studies seriously and to put an appropriate amount of effort into my academic preparation. I knew that I needed to make constructive changes to my behavior in order to correct my bad habits in school. Instead of sitting in the back of the class, I sat up front. I asked questions in class if something confused me rather than not asking. At this point in my life, I wasn't embarrassed, and I knew if something confused me, then there was a good possibility that someone else in the class was just as confused as me. If I needed help, I would see a tutor. I also knew I was a procrastinator at heart and overnight cram sessions did not help me understand the subjects I was studying. Because of this, I designated specific hours of study throughout the week for me to achieve a fair balance of school, work and personal time. I was dedicated to learning what I was being taught and to absorb as much of the material as I could.

The results of my reformed learning strategies and motivations were positive. I was enthusiastic about college, and I was not consumed with what my experience *should* be or how it *ought* to play out. I knew I would get out of college exactly what I put into it. I was making straight As, but that wasn't my ultimate goal. I viewed success in college as being able to absorb the material and being dedicated to achieving a better understanding of the subject that was being

Aurora Alexander

taught. The grades were merely a reflection of that absorption.

I was prospering in college under my new definition of success, and my confidence continued to increase throughout my college career. Focusing on the process of learning rather than staying consumed with the results allowed me to become a better student. I enjoyed the progression of my own student development instead of begrudging the reality of my college experience. This opened a new world of possibilities and everything seemed within reach, which was a far cry from where I had been when I first started out on my journey through higher education. I carried this new definition of success throughout the rest of my educational path.

● ● ●

The main conclusion I draw from my own developmental journey in college would be that reality can differ greatly from expectations. However, it doesn't mean that the entire experience is negative or that it isn't an experience worth having. Although I had suffered demoralizing failures, I was still capable of reflection, which ultimately led to my growth as a person, inside and outside the classroom. These failures and struggles were all character-building experiences that led to a revision of my personal definition of success. By acknowledging my shortcomings, I could overcome obstacles like never before. I have become very effective at identifying and mitigating problems I would have previously tried to ignore. My personal experiences as a college student have deeply impacted my beliefs of how college students develop

Aurora Alexander

by showing me that college involves learning more than what is in a book. It is more than just educational learning, it is *life* learning.

The college experience is about learning who you are as a student and as a person. You may not struggle like I did during your first year of college. You may transition into college life seamlessly, which, only means that your personal journey of development may have to come from another source other than academic struggles. However, personal growth and student development can be achieved through a multitude of circumstances related to the college experience. Whether it is learning a specific subject in a classroom or learning from different cultures by looking at yourself and others through different lenses, you are capable of growth and personal development. The context of that growth is a distinctive journey based upon the personal experiences of each individual college student, which ultimately leads to the development of their own unique definition of success. This success will lead you to a career path that is based on your own interests and internal motivations.

So, now ask yourself the hard questions. Are your plans and decisions based on reality or fantasy? How did you come to choose your future career field? Did you use reliable sources? Do you know how to study? I mean, *really* know how to study? What is motivating you to do well in school? The thing to keep in mind is that it's okay to change your major. It's okay to switch career goals, but you need to be intentional about your moves. Basing your career goals off a movie, a TV show, or your interests is not enough. You want to make well-informed decisions about your future. Do some investigative reporting by conducting field research in your potential career field.

Hopefully you won't need an icepack to reduce the swelling from that reality slap. But, I can probably guess what you are thinking right about now.

Where do I even start? Who can I talk to about this? I need some guidance. I wish that there was someone that I could rely on to help guide the way.

Lucky for you, there is such a person. You just need to look in the right spot. You'll need an academic advisor to help you navigate this tricky path through school.

One Page Memo–It's Not Like the Movies

I can choose a major/career based on my favorite movie or TV show, right? WRONG! Fantasy vs. Reality! The Real job is not nearly as glamorous or is it?

Who, What, When, Where, Why and How on Mastering this Memo

- **How?** Take classes within the field, ask questions to individuals that work in the field and research online
- **What?** Separate fantasy from reality
- **When?** As soon as possible!
- **Who?** Contact academic advisors, instructors, faculty advisors and individuals within the career field
- **Where?** Everywhere and anywhere within your field of interest!
- **Why?** Because if you are going to switch majors, you'll want to do it before it's too late

Make well-informed decisions about your future by conducting investigative reporting through field research in your potential career field.

Actively start separating the fantasy from the reality and analyze motivational factors for a specific major/career:

- Interests
- Mentors
- High school experiences
- Parents
- Teachers
- Other life experiences

YOUR MEMO – Not Like the Movies

- What is your major?

- How did you pick this major?

- How did you research this major?

- What job/career field do you ultimately want?

- Have you talked to anyone who currently works in the field?

- What job would you like to shadow for the day?

- Where on campus can you find information about internships?

MEMO NOTES

Memo #2

Academic Advising

"Dig the well before you are thirsty." – Chinese Proverb

When you were a kid, did you ever dig a hole in the sand at the beach? I did plenty of times. However, my attempts at digging a hole at the beach were really an afterthought. I never appropriately prepared for the dig. My thoughts were totally consumed with just getting to the ocean and the sand. I never really stopped to think about what I needed to prepare.

Swimsuit? Check. Towel? Check. Sunscreen? Who cares?

Side note: EVERYONE NEEDS SUNSCREEN! This is just one of the many tips from Baz Luhrmann's song "Everybody's Free (To Wear Sunscreen.)"[8] It's science, people. Protect yourself. But as a child, I couldn't have cared less. *Don't miss the sunscreen memo like I did.* I only thought about the bare necessities. I didn't even take a moment to consider that I might like to play with some toys at the beach.

When you're at the beach, it's easy to find sand toys at those little touristy beach shops for cheap. The toys usually come in little bundles covered with netting. Most of these bundles are the same: small sand pail, a rake, a sand sifter and the most important piece, the shovel. If you're going to dig a hole, you're going to need a shovel. Using your hands is a convenient alternative because they are just there. However, after a while in the sun, your hands get tired. You could also use a spoon, but that's dumb. If you were spending the day on the beach with some of your friends, how weird would it be if your friend pulled out a spoon to dig in the sand? Everyone's reaction would be the same. *What a total weirdo!* Even though it's used for scooping too, we know that a spoon is not nearly as effective as a shovel. You need a shovel for this kind of job. A tool that is used for digging, lifting and moving bulk materials. You need a tool to do heavy lifting.

If I had put an ounce of thought into planning my day at the beach, I would have definitely brought a shovel. The key word to that statement was "planning." If I had only planned for my adventure, I would have been adequately prepared. Planning is one of the most important, if not *the* most important part of any process when working towards a goal. Getting a degree in college? You definitely must take time to plan for the road ahead.

I'm sure in school you heard about the tallest mountain in the world. Everyone has heard about Mount Everest and the people who go on expeditions hoping to attain the biggest achievement ever by climbing to the top of the mountain. It's true that there have been people to successfully climb Mount Everest, but many adventurers have failed. Many people that attempt this magnificent feat quit before they make it to the top. The few individuals who make it to the top are never alone. They have considerable help from expert guides called Sherpas.

Sherpas are an ancient group of mountain-dwelling people who live in Nepal. Positioned in the shadows of the great mountain is the Khumba Valley that is inhabited by thousands of Sherpa families. Even though the word "Sherpa" translates to "easterner," westerners have recently adopted the term in a more modern sense to mean someone who is an expert that helps guide others along the tricky terrain in the professional world. Much like the cluster of Sherpa families, academic advisors dwell within the slippery terrain of the university.

There's no better way to plan for your educational journey than with the help of an academic advisor. The academic advisor will show you the proper tools you will need to possess to achieve your goal of graduating from college. An academic advisor is like a cultural Sherpa, a mountaineering expert that guides you on your path to reach the summit of your college education.

Academic advisors are on campus to provide humane guidance to outsiders. In this scenario, academic advisors are assistants who know more than the boss. You are the boss of your destiny. Academic advisors are the assistants who guide you through the social landscape of your college education, by safely shepherding you to the summit of your destiny.

Why are academic advisors important? Much like Sherpas, most people could not reach the summit, attain the ultimate goal, without the help of a guide who specializes in navigating through college. Kent Cool, an eleven-time Everest climber, said, "The Sherpas are so important. For one, they're the local people, so they know the culture, they know the area, they know the people."[9] The same can be said for academic advisors. Who would know the people, the paths and the culture of college better than someone who dwells within its domain? Academic advisors help get the logistics in place, and they are the backbone of any educational expedition. Remember, academic advisors are there to lighten your load when you are weary, encourage you to keep walking when you want to stop, and to remind you of your educational and professional goals. Many goals can be accomplished, but nobody does it alone.

More often than not, students walk into my office empty-handed. No pen and no paper. When I see this, I assume the student thinks this appointment is just a required box that needs to be checked every semester. The *lets-get-this-over-with* attitude is clear. That's probably because it's called "Required Advising." It's hard to shake the negative connotation that the phrase evokes. Something that is "required" can seem like a chore. Who looks forward to doing a chore? *Uh... not me!* I meet with students every day with a similar mindset.

• • •

Jasmine came into my office on the verge of quitting school. In fact, she said she was ready to quit life. She said she worked full-time and went to school full-time. She felt as if there was no end in sight to her bachelor's degree. She felt pressure from her family to finish. Jasmine was the oldest in the family, and she had brothers and sisters looking up to her as a role model. She was a first-generation student, and her parents had dreams of her getting her four-year degree. Jasmine was tired and wanted to give up. She felt as if she were spinning her wheels in her academic journey. I looked over Jasmine's requirements and saw she was only three semesters away from graduating.

When Jasmine realized how close she was to the finish line, her hope was renewed. She saw that all her hard work was paying off. Seeing she was so close didn't take away the fact she was tired, but it gave her the encouragement she needed to finish strong. I met with Jasmine each semester before she graduated. Each time I saw increasingly more joy in her eyes. She was so excited for her future. She expressed that if she hadn't met with me for academic advising when she did, then she would have dropped out of school. Meeting with an academic advisor and making a plan allowed Jasmine to see that her hopes and dreams were in sight. Her story reminded me of my struggle in school.

● ● ●

When I was in the middle of my bachelor's degree, academic advising was not a requirement. Now, many colleges require students to meet with an academic advisor each semester. This policy was no doubt instituted because of students just like me. To say I struggled in college is an understatement. I fancied myself a "jack-of-all-trades." I thought I could be a great many things. Therefore, I had a hard time focusing in on a major that best fit my interests. At home, I would watch a TV show or a movie that would introduce a specific profession to me. I could envision myself doing exactly what the characters were doing. Their lives on the screen seemed so intriguing. I thought, "I could totally do that." And just like that...I would change my major without ever consulting an advisor. Then I would schedule those classes within the major only to figure out I was actually disinterested in the subject and unmotivated to do well in the courses.

Becoming disenchanted with yet another major, I would consult family and close friends. They would ask about my strengths. I always enjoyed writing. It came naturally. Numbers never made sense, but words were a tool I understood well. Because of this, my mother's knee-jerk reaction to my problem was to suggest journalism. The skill of writing was effortless for me, but would it be something I could see myself doing as a profession? I got scared with all the many choices at my fingertips. I went with my mom's suggestion because I thought success would come a little easier for me in this profession considering I was "naturally gifted." I again enrolled into a semester's worth of courses in a major that didn't motivate me. I continued on this path for years, repeating the same pattern... hastily choose a major, take a semester of classes, get frustrated in the courses, either receive a D or F or ultimately withdraw from the class to receive a W on my transcript.

I was making these decisions without the guidance of an academic advisor. I knew they existed, but I didn't really see their relevance. To be quite honest, I saw the position of an academic advisor as a glorified class scheduler. *Why should I make my appointment weeks in advance to see someone that will look at the major's road map to tell me what classes I need to take for next semester? What's the point? I can do that myself.* I did not take into consideration the wealth of information that an academic advisor has in their arsenal.

After seven years, at least 10 official major changes and several semesters on hiatus, I saw an academic advisor. Her name was Joan, and she was a no-nonsense kind of woman. She had three desks in her office, pushed together in a C-shape with stacks of students' files sitting on each edge of the desks. The room was little more than an enclosed cubicle. She voluntarily kept the lights dim in the office with one lamp that shined on pictures of her family. She pulled my file, looked at it and then looked at me. I could only imagine what she was thinking at this point. Saying that my transcripts were *eclectic* was a generously forgiving thought. After years of bouncing from one major to the next and not caring about any of my classes, my grades had sunk to an all-time low of a 1.8 GPA. I was on academic probation. One more semester like that, I would be thrown out of school and I would not have the support of financial aid. I was truly scared that I had carelessly thrown away my opportunity for getting a college education.

"How can I help you?" she said as she peered over her reading glasses at me. "I want to know what I need to do to turn this around," I said with determination. "This?" she scoffed, knowing exactly what I meant. "Yes, this. My grades. As you can see from my transcripts, I'm on academic probation."

I told her that my goal was to eventually go to graduate school, but that I wasn't exactly sure which program. As I sat on the chair, waiting for her answer, I white-knuckled my notebook in an effort to calm my nerves and to brace myself for the worst. Again, she looked at me, flipped through my transcripts and then looked back at me. With a sigh, she said, "Graduate school? That will be a stretch." With more determination in my voice, I said, "What do I need to do?" She took her glasses off and folded them together as she laid them down on her desk. The woman looked me straight in the eyes. Without blinking she told me I would have to repeat a solid year of courses. As she saw it, it was the only way I could make an attempt at pulling my grades up enough to be considered for a graduate program. Oddly, I was okay with that response. I immediately thought of that scene in the movie *Dumb and Dumber* where Lloyd Christmas says, "So you're telling me there's a chance?"[10]

From that point on in my undergraduate studies, I no longer picked classes willy-nilly, based on whims. Each semester I would develop a game-plan with my advisor to correct my mistakes and to get myself back on track. Even though I was repeating classes because I had either failed them or withdrew from them, I felt in control of my destiny. I was no longer insecure about my past or nervous about the future. I had someone showing me the different paths and helping me choose the route that made the most sense for my career goals. Then I truly understood the role of an academic advisor and why they were necessary for students. I thought to myself, "If only I would have known this my freshman year...who knows where I would be now."

Depending on your college, you may or may not be required to see an academic advisor every semester. At my university, it is a requirement for nearly every student to see an academic advisor before they can register for classes. There is a hold put on the student's account until they meet with an advisor to discuss their progression through the semester, to talk about upcoming requirements and to outline courses for the next semester. If it is not a requirement to meet with an academic advisor every semester, it should be. You NEED to talk with a professional before you register for classes next semester. Things happen. Goals change. It's best to see someone to discuss these changes in detail.

Look at these advising appointments each semester as pit stops in a race. The long road to graduation is like a NASCAR race. Pit stops are needed for refueling. The same concept can apply to your educational journey. You need to stop in every semester to talk with an academic advisor to refuel for the journey ahead. In NASCAR, you may need maintenance on your vehicle. New tires or repairs on the car are just some things that can be performed on these pit stops. These mechanical adjustments are needed to finish the race. Why would your educational journey be any different? You will need to make adjustments to your plans along the way.

In NASCAR, it's not just about the driver. There is an entire pit team devoted to the success of the driver. The pit team's strategy is not set in stone. The strategy is flexible and subject to change depending on the unpredictable events that can happen during a race. Make your academic advisor your pit crew captain for your race to the finish line. Come in every semester for a pit stop to make sure you are on track to graduation. If anything pops up that may cause a problem in your journey, stop in to see your academic advisor to immediately recalculate the race strategy and optimize the time you have remaining in your degree program. Your academic advisor is there to help you make it to your degree on the other side of the finish line.

Academic advisors are FREE. Use them to your advantage in school. It may be a requirement for you to see one, but don't dismiss it as a chore. This is an opportunity for you to talk about your thoughts on your major. I can definitely see how a student could see this mandatory visit as a barrier to scheduling courses. However, if you can do a mind shift to re-frame the concept, you might look forward to these appointments. Try viewing these advising appointments like pit stops on your journey through school.

Advising appointments are also like rest stops,

because who doesn't love to take a quick break on a long road trip? *Am I right?* On a real road trip, a rest stop is an opportunity for you to stretch your legs and take a deep breath of open air; all the while you are preparing for your next leg of the trip. It's also the perfect opportunity for you to refresh, refuel and recharge. Your educational journey is no different. Think of your appointment with your academic advisor as a chance to stretch your mental legs. You can reflect over your progress in the semester, answer questions, make adjustments to next steps to future goals and get encouragement to finish your semester strong.

Once you have found your guide on campus to help you navigate the educational terrain, it is time for you to consider exploring the world. Literally. There are so many different resources at your fingertips to see how other people live and to immerse yourself in another culture. This will help broaden your horizons and open your eyes to the world outside your zip code. What are these resources and where do you find them, you may ask? I can answer that question with a little joke. What did the stamp say to the envelope? *Stick with me kid, I'll take you places.*

One Page Memo – Academic Advising

Academic Advising: I can just follow the roadmap, right? WRONG! With any long journey, you will need to have an expert guide (academic advisor) and make plenty of pit stops (advising appointments) along the way.

Who, What, When, Where, Why and How on Mastering this Memo

- **How?** Google your institution's name and academic advising within your college/department/major/minor
- **What?** See what comes up for your institution and specific college/department/major/minor
- **When?** Office hours and services
- **Who?** Name of contact person (Advisor) and/or contact information (email and phone)
- **Where?** Office location
- **Why?** An academic advisor is the free assistant to help guide you.

Think of appointments with academic advisors as pit stops to reflect on your progress, answer questions and adjust for future goals.

Contact the Academic Advising Office at your college or in your department to find out about:

- Scheduled appointments
- Online resources
- Walk-in advising hours
- How-to guides and videos
- Peer advisors
- Programs and workshops

YOUR MEMO – Academic Advising

What is the name of your academic advisor?

Where is their office located on campus?

Is it required for you to meet with an advisor every semester?

How far in advance can you make an appointment?

What job would you like to shadow for the day?

Where on campus can you find information about internships?

Do you have a road map for your major?

What are some questions that you could ask your academic advisor the next time that you meet? List 3 questions.

MEMO NOTES

Memo #3

Study Abroad

"Twenty years from now you will be more disappointed by the things you didn't do than by the ones you did do." – Mark Twain

Matthew came in to see me to ask questions about the study abroad program. He said he wanted to go but was wondering if he really could do it. He said he was also nervous about traveling. He admitted that he had never traveled outside the United States. As Matthew spoke, I wondered how I could persuasively encourage this student to take a chance without scaring him to death.

I meet with students every day who inquire about study abroad. Study abroad is an important program in today's university. You have the opportunity of immersing yourself

Aurora Alexander

into a culture for a set period of time while earning college credit. I'm not gonna lie to you. There are potential obstacles and challenges to study abroad.

How do I eloquently tell Matthew to take advantage of study abroad opportunities now while he is in college before it is too late?

My goal was to convey a sense of urgency, so he would look at study abroad through a lens of deep consideration. However, I was afraid that my words may send him running out of the room screaming.

Matthew went on about how he didn't know if he would be up to staying away from his family. *If he thinks he has a family now, just wait until he has some screaming babies at home and mouths to feed.* He was concerned about his obligations here at college and didn't know if he could make it work considering he has a part-time job and lives in the dorms. *I wouldn't consider those obligations. Those sound more like easy outs.*

The financial piece was also a concern for Matthew. I explained that if money was an issue that sometimes there were certain scholarships awarded to individuals who are looking for study abroad opportunities. *Just wait until the weight of supporting a household and paying bills presses down on your shoulders.* During the appointment, we discussed how the study abroad programs differ in length. If Matthew didn't want to stay away from his friends and family for a semester, he could capitalize on other opportunities through the study abroad program. The study abroad office at our university offered many options for students including a full year, semester-long, one month, alternative spring breaks and Christmas vacation programs. I encouraged him to reach out to study abroad to find out more information.

My goal of this meeting with Matthew was simple. I wanted him to fully consider the benefits of taking advantage of study abroad opportunities. I also wanted him to understand the reality of life after college without sending him into anaphylactic shock. I've seen life hit people like a severe allergic reaction. With no EpiPens in sight, I knew I needed to give him the truth in a delicate manner. At no point did I ever dismiss Matthew's concerns, because they were real to *him*. I encouraged Matthew to not dismiss the study abroad program based on his fears. I stressed to him he would find it beneficial to do his own research about the different study abroad programs that were offered. That way he could face his fears head-on with facts.

I met with Matthew the following semester. He was proud to say he was going to Florence, Italy to study abroad, on *his* terms. He was going for a summer institute that lasts one month. He was happy that he could find something that allowed him to visit another culture without making the semester-long commitment. Matthew's concerns reminded me of my concerns when I was considering study abroad in college.

• • •

There is definitely a timing issue that is worth discussing. So, I will be frank. Freshman year is crazy! College life is a totally different reality than high school. Even if you have taken advantage of early college programs where you take college courses during high school, it's still a complete change. A lot of students will live away from home for the first time. You will be forced to do a lot

Aurora Alexander

of things that are outside of your comfort zone.

Let's just take a second to consider a hypothetical situation, shall we? Maybe you think it won't be that big of a change because you are that rare, one-in-a-million student that is super independent. Maybe you always did your own laundry at home. Mommy never washed your clothes. No one ever had to tell you that you needed to do a load of laundry. You always folded and put away your clothes nicely and neatly. Your clean clothes never spent over five minutes in a laundry basket. You are the only person you know who never scrambled at the last minute to find clean underwear. You were and are totally self-sufficient with your wardrobe. If this sounds like you, you deserve a medal because I still don't live up to these standards. And, unfortunately for you, there will still be a certain level of change you will face when starting college.

You will need to figure out where you will do your laundry. Where are you going to store your laundry detergent? Are you going to save money and take your clothes home on the weekends or are you going to spend the money to do them on campus? Does your dorm have a laundry facility or will you have to go off campus? Where would that be located? What are the hours of operation? Can you do your laundry between classes or will you have to do it at the end of the day? I could keep going with more questions, but I will spare you at this point because I'm sure you are sensing a pattern. This little exercise was to show you that no matter how prepared you think you are, you are in for a change.

This is not just about laundry, by the way. You will have

to adjust to everything. Where will you sleep? Where are your classes? Who are *your* people? Where will you meet these people? Where will you eat? Should you join any clubs? *YES!* Your freshman year will be spent trying to find homeostasis. By the end of your second semester on campus, you should have it figured out for the most part. So, studying abroad freshman year might not be the best choice to set you up for success. Let's take a minute to explore alternative times.

As you progress through school, things will become increasingly normal. You will understand how things work in your new life and you will take on new experiences and some new responsibilities. You'll have different goals as you transition through class levels. In your junior year, you should be thinking about the light at the end of the tunnel. (Getting a job or getting into graduate school!) You should add experiences outside the classroom to gain useful knowledge about your intended career field by taking advantage of research labs, internships and/or volunteering opportunities.

By the time your senior year rolls around, you should have your eyes on the prize. (Find a job or getting into a graduate program.) You'll be so busy jumping through flaming hoops to cross that finish line you might not have an opportunity to even breathe. You'll be so focused on the next chapter that studying abroad at this point might seem a little out of step. Many students have created so much momentum to carry them to their specific goals it may seem counterintuitive to spend their final months in college in a different country.

Aurora Alexander

That's why I think it's best to travel abroad in the second semester of your sophomore year. My standard rule of thumb is figure out your *new* normal freshman year and travel the world your sophomore year. *Why the second semester of my sophomore year?* I'm glad you asked. Even though you already had an entire year to figure out your new normal in college as a freshman, there still might be some kinks to work out like learning how to juggle a new job or fitting in time to see a new significant other. Sophomore year is a good time for you to explore past what you already know.

Keep in mind that the second-semester sophomore suggestion is only that, a suggestion. The Study Abroad office would go out of business if students only chose the spring semester. However, based on my personal experience and my experience with students, the spring semester of the second year seems to be a nice time to slide in an opportunity to immerse yourself into another culture for an extended period. However, there are always exceptions. Some students are required to study abroad due to the major's curriculum programming. For example, my institution requires students within the fashion major to study abroad for one semester. The courses you need to take in the fashion major before going abroad are in lock-step and require planning ahead of time to successfully fulfill all the requirements. So, the timing of all of this might not exactly align with a second-semester sophomore status.

In another case, students on a pre-med track might not do a traditional study abroad program their sophomore year because programs like that are highly sequential. Meaning, a student needs to do *this* before *that*, before *this*, before *that*. If you miss one class in the sequence, it could throw off your whole program by a semester or worse. Student-athletes also struggle with this because their seasons, classes and schedules for practice and travel are made so far in advance, there is virtually no option for them during their sophomore year.

If you fall into one of these categories where the second semester of your sophomore year makes little sense or will put you behind, you DO have options. I have worked with many students who have done study abroad in other semesters other than the second semester of their sophomore year. The reason for this, however, was because a full semester program didn't gel with them. Who can blame them? Choosing to live in a different country, culture, and environment for an extended period is not an easy decision to make. After much consideration and research, these students could take advantage of alternative study abroad programs that better fit their lifestyles.

• • •

My personal story with study abroad boils down to flirting with the idea of going abroad, but never pulling the trigger. *I sound like a total Debbie Downer. Cue the sad sound effect.* (Womp… Womp) Study abroad seemed as exotic as space exploration to me. I found it fascinating, yet wildly absurd. In my mind, the thought of me living in another country for a semester was as far-fetched as me living on Mars for a semester. My brain just couldn't make sense of such a ludicrous notion.

I was a first-generation student. For those of you

who do not know what that means, I was a student whose parents never went to college. Going to college was already a stretch. My dad raised an eyebrow at the idea of me going. He was a coal miner, and we lived in a poverty-stricken area in the coalfields of West Virginia. Most people did not go to college in my area. However, my mom told me from a young age that her expectations of me included a college education. From the age of 4 or 5 years old, I was told that I needed to get a degree. My whole life, I knew going to college was the ultimate goal.

No family or friends had ever gone away to college. As I mentioned before, I had seen people on TV and movies go to college, but never someone I knew in real life. A lot of my family didn't even finish high school. My mom dropped out of the 8th grade when she got pregnant with me at fourteen. All the men in my family, including my father, were coal miners. I did not come from a family of financial means by any stretch of the imagination. Going to college for me was a stretch, socially and economically. I felt the full weight of the burden on my shoulders the minute I received college advertisements in the mail during my senior year in high school.

Carrying that burden with me onto campus was hard enough, but then I heard about the opportunities of studying abroad. As I mentioned before, just like space travel, I was fascinated and intrigued by the concept of study abroad. I remember walking into the student center at my school and seeing that the study abroad office was doing a presentation on some of their locations. I sat down to listen for a bit. *There's no harm in just listening, right?*

They talked about their study abroad program in New Zealand. Of all the places in the world, New Zealand never crossed my mind as a place I would even consider visiting. However, the pictures that were shown, the videos of other students exploring the stunning landscapes and the courses that were offered there were so enticing. New Zealand sounded magical. I mean, it is where the Lord of the Rings trilogy was filmed. *What's more magical than hobbits and wizards?[11]*

The Study Abroad office presentation included the Waitomo Glowworm Caves. They showed pictures and video of students who went tubing through these black water caves. But these weren't just ordinary caves. The ceiling of the caves is covered with thousands of little glowworms, Arachnocampa Luminosa, which are unique to New Zealand, making the cave ceiling look like the starry night sky. (Google it! You won't regret it.) To a backwoods country girl, whose role model was Sally Ride, the first American female in space, this sounded like an attainable adventure. This was *my* chance at space travel.

I walked out of that presentation with a surge of energy I hadn't felt in a long time. It inspired me about the opportunity to study abroad in New Zealand. I raced home to tell my mom. I told her all about the study abroad presentation, New Zealand, the caves and the glowworms. I spared no detail. After an animated retelling of the story, my mom's reaction did not mirror mine. She said, "Oh that sounds nice." My enthusiasm was immediately deflated. I will not lie, I was super bummed. I thought she would be just as enchanted as I was with this opportunity and when she wasn't, all the wind was sucked out of my sails.

At this point in my life, my parents had gotten a divorce. My mom's new normal was that she was living life as a single-mom and working full-time. She had also decided in this season of her life that she wanted to go to college to change careers. (Weirdly, we were enrolled at the same college at the same time. We even took some classes together.) Meanwhile, I was a young college student who was working part-time and going to school. Every month was a struggle for us. I know exactly what my mom was thinking. *That sounds nice and all, but I don't think you can afford that.*

Okay, so, my mom was coming from a place of concern, right? I can't hold that against her. I decided at this point to pitch this idea to my friends. I wanted to know what they would think about extraordinary opportunity. I ran it by some of my coworkers. I explained to them how magical New Zealand sounded. I talked about the caves and the glowworms. I was looking for them to match my intrigue in this adventure. Somehow my coworkers were just as underwhelmed by the New Zealand conversation as my mom. *How could this be?* New Zealand sounded amazing! I couldn't understand their lack of enthusiasm.

Out of frustration, I made a trusty pros and cons list. I immediately started on the pros list. I wrote, "Sounds awesome–Once in a lifetime!" Then I wrote something in the cons list. *Ya know, to equal it out.* Once I started on the cons list, I couldn't stop. It was astonishing how quickly I filled up the cons side. Here are just some things I listed.

Aurora Alexander

- Too expensive

- How would I pay my bills while I'm away?

- Who would take care of my cat?

- Would I still have my job when I came back?

- Is this really educational or is it just for fun?

- Is this needed or is this a luxury?

- Homesick?

I took a moment to sit back and analyze my list. The mismatch between the pros and cons was staggering. I had this long list of reasons not to go. Yet, I could only think of one reason to go. It crushed me. I kept that list on my nightstand for over a year. I looked at it occasionally when I was thinking about the New Zealand presentation and the glowworms. I would look at the pros, or shall I say, pro (singular). Then I would quickly glance at the cons. That would take the wind out of my sails again and I would quickly put the list back down on my nightstand.

As you can probably imagine, I never went to New Zealand. I look back now, years later, and I'm still confused as to why I could not act. Was it fear? Was it the heavy weight of reality I was carrying with me? Or maybe it was a little of both? Whatever the combination, it was a deadly dose. I allowed factors like these to sway many of my big life decisions. I'll never know if I did the right thing.

It's difficult to think about all the opportunities I neglected to take advantage of when they were at my fingertips. However, there is a silver lining in all of this. I deeply appreciate travel now. I make it a priority in my life to this day. I can see now I missed out on some memorable moments because of my fears.

The good news is that I did end up traveling a little when I was in college. However, it was not with a study abroad program. Fortunately for me, my best friend, Krista, and I were able to spend some time in Europe thanks in part to her family. Although I am happy that I went and it was a life-changing opportunity, the experience was not nearly long enough. I was only there for ten days. Ten days are better than no days in my opinion, but it wasn't a study abroad program. I still feel regret about not exploring the opportunities within the various study abroad programs that were available to me. Because of this, New Zealand is still on my bucket list to this day. In the words of Susan Sontag, an American writer, and filmmaker, "I haven't been everywhere, but it's on my list."[12]

● ● ●

I believe a decision like whether to study abroad comes down to a level of maturity. Not only should you have the insight to know if you should go, but also have the foresight of knowing when you should go. Think of a baby. (No, I do not look at students as babies. This is the most general analogy I can think of at the moment.) Babies have to crawl before they walk, right? Before babies can crawl, they need to have the strength and balance to get up on all fours, correct? The same concept can be applied to study abroad. But there are always exceptions.

Now I work in higher education, I know that Study Abroad Offices offer so many options for students. There are different programs and program lengths, so there are varying costs associated with the different programs. There are full year or semester-long programs. They offer summer institutes where a student will only be gone for a month. Most Study Abroad offices even have alternative spring breaks and Christmas break programs for students who don't want to commit to an extended stay. These shorter programs are considerably less money and more of an economical choice for students who are considering studying abroad.

If there is any chance that you will look back and regret missing the opportunity to study abroad, *and* if you have the maturity, foresight, and schedule to allow it, just go for it. Make it happen and enjoy the experience.

One Page Memo – Study Abroad

Study Abroad: Should I or shouldn't I?

If you are slightly interested in the idea of study abroad, it doesn't hurt to ask the experts.

Who, What, When, Where, Why and How on Mastering this Memo

- **How?** Google your institution's name and study abroad
- **What?** See what comes up for your institution
- **When?** Presentations and/or office hours
- **Who?** Name of contact person (Coordinator/Advisor) and/or contact information (email and phone)
- **Where?** Office location and location of upcoming events
- **Why?** If you don't ask, you'll never know, right?

See the world, expand your horizons, hone language skills, explore possible career opportunities, find new interests and embrace personal development.

Contact your college's Study Abroad Office to find out about:

- Available programs
- Destinations
- Scholarship opportunities
- Testimonials from students
- Viable options
- Range of costs associated with study abroad

YOUR MEMO – Study Abroad

- Where would you like to travel?

- Does your major/dept./college have a program?

- Where is your Study Abroad office?

- Contact information and office hours?

- What programs/places to do they offer?

- Are there scholarships available?

- What does the application process look like?

- If you studied abroad, how long would you like to go?

MEMO NOTES

Memo #4

Experience

"The only source of knowledge is experience." Albert Einstein.

      In this memo, I'm going to jump ahead a little in my life story. I'll give you the SparkNotes version for context. I ended up graduating with my bachelor's degree. I knew that I wanted to work in the counseling field in some way, which would require me to get into a graduate school program. I decided that I wanted to get my master's in counseling. I started applying to a few of those programs. The graduate school application process was very complex. For a first generation student, the experience was totally overwhelming to me. I was the epitome of a fish out of water.

Aurora Alexander

Remember how stressful it was when you were applying to college? Well, triple it! THAT is what it's like when applying for graduate school. Instead of jumping through three or four hoops to get into college, you now have to jump through TEN hoops. Oh...and did I forget to mention? Those hoops are on fire! It can be mentally and emotionally draining.

After submitting my application to a particular counseling program, I was called in to do a graduate admissions interview as part of the application process. If I had a successful interview, my information would then be presented to a panel of individuals within the program to decide if I was to be accepted into the master's-level program. So, I needed to impress all sorts of people to get into graduate school, on paper and in person. There was a lot riding on this interview and I knew it.

During my admissions interview for graduate school, I noticed that the admissions committee kept asking me the same question. They asked me, "How do you know you want this program?" This question confused me because I thought it was obvious. *Hello?!? I'm not here to waste my time, energy and money on something I don't want.* I didn't say that to them, but I was thinking it. It wasn't an accident I had chosen a counseling program. I didn't pick it by throwing darts at a board. I genuinely had an interest in the field. Unfortunately, my answer didn't seem to quench their curiosity. The line of questioning became increasingly insistent. "How do we know that you will like it?" they continued. Clearly, I wasn't picking up what they were laying down. They finally asked, "How do we know that you won't get into the program and quit after a semester or two because this isn't what you were expecting?"

Before my graduate school interview, I truly thought I had it in the bag. I am a likable person. Not to brag, but I'm actually quite charming when I need to be. I had always succeeded in prior interview experiences before. So, why would an interview for graduate school be any different? I wasn't too worried beforehand. I was going in prepared and ready to talk about myself in a positive light. My sense of humor usually defaults into self-deprecation, but I knew I needed to curb that during the interview. Even though I had struggled in my undergraduate degree, I knew how to talk about my experience in a professional manner that showed grace and growth. I knew I needed to focus on what I had learned from my missteps rather than dwelling on the mistakes themselves. I was well rehearsed in glossing over the mistakes and putting a positive spin on the results.

I had a pretty good story. I was very passionate about why I wanted to get into the program and counseling field. My reasoning behind my choice was very thoughtfully explained and supported with relevant facts. They could see that my decision to pursue a career in the field of counseling was a well-informed decision and not a whim.

Luckily, they let me into the program. However, their line of questioning still left me confused well into my first semester of graduate school. *Why were they so insistent on hammering me with those questions?* I couldn't understand.

As the semester unfolded, I made friends with the other students in my cohort. They were individuals from varying backgrounds. Some of them had just graduated with their bachelor's degrees while others had worked real-world jobs for 10-15 years before coming back to school. My friend, Clay, graduated with a degree in psychology and had done a ton of research while pursuing his bachelor's degree. My other friend, Katie, had a similar background, but she had interned at a rape crisis center for a couple of years. Matthew had worked in the field as a case manager for the state government. Christina had started a soup kitchen at her church, which helped the underprivileged in the community. The backgrounds of these individuals were very impressive. It got me thinking. As I took an inventory of my cohort and comparing myself to their experiences, I realized something huge.

The admissions committee was gambling on me!

The individuals that allowed me into the counseling program were taking a chance on me because I was coming from a completely random background. I didn't have a degree relevant to counseling. I never stepped foot inside a research lab. I never had an internship. I had never worked in the field before or used the relevant skills needed for counseling. I had volunteered in the past, but nothing recent. To the counseling program, I was a wild card. My interest in counseling and helping people was coming out of left field.

Believe it or not, I wasn't an idiot. I knew what the word "internship" meant, but I didn't realize how much weight it carried. Until that point, I didn't understand the importance of experience outside the classroom, whether it is research, internship, volunteering or working in the field. What it shows to people is that you have an intention. That is why they were hammering me on my intention because they couldn't see it.

Stepping your foot into the water with a bit of experience, no matter how small you think it is, shows investment. Having experience under your belt can help you with direction and give you some purpose in your endeavors. This is what I was lacking. On paper, my direction and purpose looked haphazard and unplanned.

After this little hiccup, I quickly appreciated the importance of experience. I could see that, ultimately, people want to work with students who show intention and thoughtfulness. There's more to school than making good grades. Once I saw the distinction, I wanted to become an *intentional* student and gain as much experience as I could while I was in school. Even though my program had an internship component embedded within the curriculum, I knew I still needed to find that experience on my own. The program did not operate as an internship placement site. I was on my own in finding an experience. The drive had to come from within.

The internship requirement involved at least 600 hours working at an internship before graduation. They usually spread these hours over two semesters. However, I wanted more. I found an internship a semester before my required internship hours started. I wanted to gain as much experience as possible. My goal was to be viewed not as an intern, but as a member of a team. I wanted to gain enough responsibility that my coworkers wouldn't see me as a student, but rather as a professional. The experience and professionalism I gained during my internships then helped guide me to where I am today. What I learned helped me make a seamless transition. Seamless transitions are always better than the alternative no matter the scenario.

• • •

Have you ever been to an airport where they have moving walkways? They are conveyer belts for humans. They are AMAZING! Every time I see one at a place, I immediately become a 6-year-old kid. It reminds of going to the grocery store with my mom when I was little.

My favorite thing to do at the store as a kid was to put the food on the conveyer belt because it was so cool. The conveyer belt does all the work. I strongly believe that is why some major airports and theme parks have these moving walkways. These human conveyor belts were deliberately developed to better serve the customer. I think the university should join the club and spring for those in some high-traffic areas on campus. A conveyer belt just makes things easier. Conveyer belts didn't happen by accident. They were strategically placed to increase customer satisfaction with seamless transitions.

In college, some majors and degree programs operate much like a conveyer belt. These conveyor belts are embedded within the program to help students reach their ultimate goal, which is a job. Everyone is familiar with these conveyer belt degrees like nursing, education, and accounting. Nursing programs produce nurses. Education programs produce teachers. Accounting programs produce accountants. These students do not have to put a lot of thought into what they want to be when they are finished with the degree. Maybe they have to wonder what type of environment they want to work in or what kind of population they would like to help, but they ultimately know they will be the profession of the program.

There is another reason these conveyer belt degrees are so attractive. It's because the experience needed to get the job is embedded within the curriculum, and most students don't even realize that it's happening. Imagine these conveyer belt degrees without the experience component. Would anyone ever higher a nurse if they had never worked in a healthcare setting? No. Would a school ever consider hiring a teacher if they had never stepped foot into a classroom as a student teacher? Never. Would a company ever consider hiring an accountant who never trained under other accountants in a professional environment? Not likely. There would be no jobs for these graduates unless they had some level of experience relevant to the field. Nursing students have clinicals. Education students have student teaching. Accountants have co-ops. These programs are designed specifically to give the students the experience that is necessary to get a job. Many students believe a degree will get you a job. Degrees do NOT equal jobs. A student needs the relevant, hands-on experience outside the classroom to help leverage themselves to get to where they want to go.

Gaining experience outside the classroom can prove more difficult for students in other majors, like the liberal arts. Many of these degrees do not require experience outside the classroom to graduate. Easily, students can cruise through their bachelor's degree and gain no real experience outside the classroom relevant to their career field. I did it. I see students do it every day. School is hard enough as it is. It is everything that a student can do to make it on the other side of their degree in one piece. A student has to strategically balance school, work, friends, family, responsibilities, and life. It's hard to imagine that someone would elect to juggle one more thing on top of their already jam-packed schedule. But it is a necessary evil.

I am a certified career coach. My training is in career advising and career counseling. I work with recruiters, hiring managers and HR personnel regularly. I am familiar with the job market and job postings. Most job postings for entry-level positions want 1-2 years' experience. Let me break this down for you. That means you already need to have experience just to get your foot into the door with an employer. As a student, I remember being confused by this concept because I was well aware of the realities in trying to land a job. *How do I get experience without experience?* It's through internships, research and volunteering opportunities. THAT is the experience employers want to see. THAT separates you from everyone else at the end of the day, not the degree.

When I'm talking with students about gaining experience, I always have them perform this exercise. You should do it too. Imagine that you are at your graduation ceremony. Your family and friends are there, the people that supported you through your entire educational journey. Everyone is so happy to see you walk across the stage and get your degree. It's a very proud moment. But take a moment to look around. You are not alone. There is a line of 150-200 students graduating with the same exact degree. What separates you from those other individuals? Your degree? Uhhh... no. We just determined that. Your minor? Nah, not really. Minors are just used as leverage to get you to where you need to go. Minors don't make you or break you when getting a job. Your grades, GPA? Well, maybe sometimes, but not really for most. If you have a 4.0 GPA and another candidate as a 2.14 GPA, you might look like a more studious individual in comparison. However, most students fall in the meaty middle, mid-3.0's to mid-2.0's. The grades don't really make or break a job opportunity either. What it boils down to is the experience piece of the puzzle.

College is not just about getting a degree. Education and experience is a 50/50 package. The classes you take, the books you read, the papers you write... etc. are only 50% of the equation. The other 50% is what you did with that information outside the classroom. Employers won't hand you a job simply because you have a piece a paper. They want to see experience. They want to see the motivation behind your decision to want to work at their company. They want to see someone who is intentional and is invested. The experience you bring to the table speaks volumes about you in a way that your degree never will. Picking a major that interests you and combining it with experience you enjoy will open opportunities you never thought possible.

I know what you are thinking. *How much experience is enough?* It depends. I always say one experience is better than none, but three experiences are better than one. Don't think of these experiences as yet another box to check off before graduation. Put thought into it. These experiences give you a glimpse of what life could be once you graduate. This is the exciting part! You try on a career for a brief moment in time to see if it is the right fit for you. Plus, it develops and fosters long-lasting connections that will prove to be meaningful to you as you become a professional. *How amazing is that?* Many students fail to see the importance of such experiences during their time in school.

● ● ●

When Brandon came in to see me for academic advising he said he was experiencing frustration over his major. He was majoring in psychology, but everyone he talked to told him he could never get a job with a psychology degree. Even though he loved his courses, he was afraid that he would be unemployed when he got out of school. He continued to tell me a story about his Uncle Bob making a big deal about his major during Thanksgiving dinner. At that point, all of Brandon's family questioned him about his major and uncertain future. *What do you want to be? What kind of work will you be qualified to do when you graduate? You mean you won't be a psychologist when you graduate with your bachelor's degree? What kind of job can you get? How will you make money? Who will hire someone with a degree like that?* Brandon's holiday break turned into a personal nightmare. He came back to school more confused than ever. He didn't know how to ease his family's legitimate concerns because he had those same thoughts and fears.

Brandon was in the middle of his junior year, and he felt he was too far into psychology to switch majors. He loved what he was studying, but he didn't want to end up unemployed and up to his eyeballs in debt. Uncle Bob had planted the seed of doubt in Brandon's mind by referring to his education as a "nothing" degree and that seed had started to take root. Questioning his past decisions and confusion about his next steps left Brandon incredibly overwhelmed. He wanted answers, but he didn't even know how to ask the questions. Luckily, I knew exactly what he was going through because I had been there before.

Over the years, I have worked with a ton of students with the same fears and questions as Brandon. It was no accident I have this job. As I mentioned before, I am a certified career coach. One reason that the Department of Psychological Sciences hired me was so I could help dispel the myth that someone with a psychology degree is unemployable. I specialize in helping students take the education they receive in the classrooms and find experiences to apply that information outside the classroom setting. *This* is how you get hired. Experience is how you find focus that will eventually lead you down the path to gainful employment.

This little thought experiment can help you make well-informed decisions about your future. Imagine you are buying shoes. Usually, you want to try on the shoes before you buy them. Now imagine your career as a pair of shoes. You will wear these shoes all day, every day for the rest of your life. You'll want to try on the career first, gain some experience to make a well-informed decision about your career.

As I mentioned before, one experience is better than none, and three experiences are better than one. There is also something else to consider. There is no such thing as a *bad* experience. The reason is that even if you don't like an experience, it still gives you information about moving forward. If you like an experience, great! If you don't, that's awesome too. Because now you know what you *don't* want. For majors where there are a multitude of career choices, it is hard to narrow down your choices. *How do I know what to choose? How do I know what I like?* That's easy! Try it on for size and see if it fits.

When I originally started my counseling program, it was for the school counseling track. I knew I wanted to work with students and I wanted to work in an educational environment. So, I naturally thought of school counseling. I really enjoyed working with children. I loved coming up with techniques for students to overcome obstacles. I also enjoyed the collaboration piece when it came to working with a student's teachers. I found that I excelled with being a liaison between these two entities. However, there was one thing that bothered me. I quickly realized that I didn't like working with parents. No matter how awesome the plan or how much the student overcame certain barriers, there was this parental component I didn't account for in the scenario. Parents could totally undermine the hard work that was happening with a student. They wouldn't do it on purpose, but it still happened. I found that aspect very frustrating. I also knew this element would be a constant reoccurrence if I stayed in the field. Because of this, I ended up switching gears and focusing on another track within my counseling program that focused on student affairs in higher education. So, I was still working with students in an educational setting, but I was working with adults who were in control of their own destinies. I very rarely have to work with parents.

If I did not have an experience to set as a baseline for my needs and wants, then I wouldn't know how to move forward. It is common for me to hear from a student who was an education major throughout school, but then they do a semester of student teaching in their senior year only to find out that they hate being a teacher. How scary is that? These students didn't know because they had never tried it. How will you know about what you want in your career unless you get your feet wet in the field through experience? Your career of choice may sound good on paper, but you may hate it in actuality because of some unknown factor you never considered. It's a real possibility that a lot of students face.

The best way to combat the unknown is by facing it head-on because you will never know unless you try it. You can do this in many ways. You could take part in research or an internship. These experiences usually only last a semester. That's relatively low on the commitment scale. Even if the experience is horrible, you can grit your teeth through anything for 16 weeks. You may not know exactly what you want, but you will know exactly what you want to avoid. This information is invaluable as you move forward in life.

Take advantage of the various levels of commitment with these experiences. Who wants to get sacked down with a big commitment when you are not even sure if you like it? Once you are in a job, you are kind of stuck at least for a period of time. Sure, you could get another job, but if you don't like the field of work, then you are in trouble. It is better to know if you like something now rather than later before it's too late. Minimal commitment is a luxury that most college students have at this point. As a college student, you could totally get away with doing an internship and never doing that kind of work again. I call them "one-and-dones." One-and-dones are great for the average college student. If you don't like it, you can just peace-out when it's over.

If a semester-long commitment is too much or not workable with your schedule, try volunteering. This is super low maintenance. Maybe you are not spending a ton of hours on site, but you are still getting a feel of how the work is done in that environment. This would be great for students who don't have a car on campus so making a commitment to be somewhere regularly off campus is not a reality just yet. You could definitely agree to volunteer somewhere every other Saturday and the 3rd Tuesday of every month. Even though it is of minimal commitment, the exposure to the field is the most important factor.

If volunteering sounds like too much, try job-shadowing. Job-shadowing is where you follow a professional around for a day or two to get a feel for their work. This is an awesome opportunity because you do not have to give a full commitment of an entire semester or summer. You are not even committing to come in regularly to volunteer your time. This is a perfect one-and-done scenario. There are plenty of jobs that sound great on paper in theory, but it's a whole different story in practice. Seeing a real professional do the not so glamorous things of their day-to-day job may be the wake-up call you need to show you that you may want something else out of your career. Whether it's the environment or the work duties or the level of respect a person receives on their job, you will get a good feel for what it would be like for you once you get into the field. If you like the experience, great! If you don't like it, move on. This is an opportunity for you to strategize, pivot, and change your career direction.

Another low-level commitment area of experience is the informational interview. (I talk about informational interviews in more detail in Memo #5: Networking) Informational interviews are *awesome* because they spare you the agony of grinding through a full semester experience or an entire day of mind-numbing work. Informational interviews allowed me the opportunity to fine tune my career choices and really hear the good, bad and ugly of the career field. As I mentioned before, something might sound great on paper, but actually seem awful to *you*. I eliminated a lot of potential areas of work by doing informational interviews. Informational interviews can last from 15 minutes to an hour. This is way less of a time suck than job shadowing or an internship. On the flip side, informational interviews opened doors for me to areas where I could then get a job shadowing opportunity or an internship. Use these informational interviews to your advantage to narrow down your choices and to make further connections within the field.

Now that you know that experience is important to your future success, next you need to think about landing that experience. Just because you know that you need experience doesn't mean that experiences are just going to fall in your lap. You have to actively go out to seek it. Wouldn't it be amazing if you had a team of people that would help you find experience? Or help you land an internship? Or help you to get into graduate school? Or help you get a job? You have to build that team and I'm going to teach you how in the next memo.

One Page Memo – Experience

How do you separate yourself from the crowd? With a degree? No. It's with experience.

Who, What, When, Where, Why and How on Mastering this Memo

- **How?** Intentionally find these experiences
- **What?** Look for experiences that require minimal commitment to try on experience
- **When?** As soon as possible!
- **Who?** Contact Career Services, academic advisors, instructors and faculty advisors for suggestions of where to look for these experiences
- **Where?** Everywhere and Anywhere!
- **Why?** You'll need experience to get into an entry-level position or graduate school, as well as narrow down your career path.

Gain experience that narrows down your potential career paths, opening doors, closing doors and showing investment within the career field. Actively start looking for opportunities outside the classroom:

- Internships
- Co-op opportunities
- Research labs
- Job-shadowing
- Conduct informational interviews

YOUR MEMO - Experience

- What experience would you like to gain?

- With what population would you like to work?

- In what kind of environment would you like to work?

- Contact information and office hours?

- Would you rather intern, do research or volunteer?

- What job would you like to shadow for the day?

- Where on campus can you find information about internships?

- Does your program have experience as a requirement?

MEMO NOTES

Memo #5

Networking

"A single conversation with a wise man is better than 10 years of study." – Chinese Proverb

I hate the word "networking." There is no way to sugar-coat my feelings about this term. It has such a negative connotation for many people. I find that it usually causes a knee-jerk reaction with most individuals. This knee-jerk reaction typically involves an eye-roll or a glossing over of the eyes, a complete tuning out of all information presented after the term "networking." It is assumed that all information from this point on will be absurdly boring.

I struggle with finding alternative terms to use instead of "networking" when I'm working with students. Professional Grooming? *That sounds mildly unsettling. Try again.* Professional Schmoozing? That has an even greasier undertone. Strategic hobnobbing? Experienced Elbow-Rubbing? *Eww, gross!* Maybe The-Term-That-Must-Not-Be-Named? At least this title would give the term a bit of intrigue. *Okay, okay... This is getting a little ridiculous now.* So, in frustration, I ultimately go back to the original term of "networking."

I have planned many networking events and networking how-to workshops. Guess who never shows up to these events and workshops? That's right...people who **need to network.** Why is that? It's because the word "networking" is social poison. I have to literally trick people to come to these events by cleverly disguising them with catchy titles because NOBODY wants to hear about networking. I know it. You know it. We all know it.

Immediately, thoughts flood into my mind of windowless rooms, with forced conversations and "Hello My Name Is..." stickers on short sleeve, button-down shirts. People exchanging awkward introductions and sweaty handshakes all while nursing a watered-down drink. Sounds exhilarating, doesn't it? *SNOOZE.* I'd rather catch my pinky toe on the corner of my coffee table than suffer through another one of *those* networking events.

It's bad enough as a professional who is established in the field of my choice. But nothing compares to the fresh hell that it was when I was a student just starting out. It was mind-numbingly awful. I'm naturally an introvert so I prefer to interact with others one-on-one or in small groups. Although I love parties and hanging out with friends and family, social events zap all of my energy. Being around too many people can drain my batteries. Networking events where I'm forced to mingle, shake hands and kiss babies like a politician can take a toll on my personality.

By the time I am broaching the "networking" subject with students, they have unquestionably taken part in a networking event already. However, these events are usually shrouded with another title to disguise its real agenda. Welcome Weekends and kick-off parties. Or anything with the words "speed" or "mixer" in it. Any event where you are forced to play icebreaker games like Human BINGO or scavenger hunts. These are ALL networking events cleverly disguised as parties. Colleges and groups try very hard to get students to network with other like-minded individuals in the hopes for you to stick around for more than one semester. It's easier to keep you here than it is to recruit a new student. That's why networking activities are always a standard at college events.

● ● ●

You, the student, should be in tune with your best interests. Not only is it necessary for you to get engaged with students and make friends with people on campus, but it's also important for you to take those same networking skills and apply them to your future goals. It's important to keep your eyes on the prize when networking. The skills that you learn at these little mixers and parties can apply to networking with professionals. The differences are that the professional connections you make will probably not help you in finding a roommate next semester. Just like, the connection you make with a student at the freshman mixer will probably not lead to your first job out of college. Both connections are important, but they are different and serve different purposes. One is a personal connection and the other is a professional connection.

The main point I want to get across to students is really the most important part. So, how can I convey to students that networking is important *NOW*? Not when you become old and grey around the temples. Not when you are in your 40s and 50s, out on the golf course. I'm talking about now while you are in school. You need to know it is imperative for you to network now while you are in school to have a leg up on your competition when you finish school. *How do I convey this to students to understand the weight that is carried with the term "networking?"*

The easiest way for me to put this into words is that networking is the number one way to get a job. (PERIOD)

Networking = #1 way to get a job.

If students can truly understand that, then they can appreciate the need for "networking." Let's face it, finding a full-time job is a full-time job. If you didn't know that little nugget of wisdom at this point in life, you'll soon figure it out. It's a daunting process to find a job. There will be a point in your life where you will wonder if you can just hire someone to find a job for you.

Networking is like playing a basketball game. Every basketball season, a coach will have the starting five for the team. These are the main, go-to people that the coach will put out onto the court when the game starts. The same idea can be applied to networking. Depending on your season in life, you will be the coach, and you will need a team of players in your corner, which consist of a starting five. The starting five for you will comprise of the top five people that will help you achieve your next goal, whether it be scoring an informational interview, job shadowing experience, internship or job.

Just like in basketball, teams just don't form. Behind the scenes, it takes a lot of time, energy and strategy to build the perfect team. This planning is done well in advance before the starting five ever steps foot onto the court for the first game. The same amount of strategy needs to be put into your starting five. First, you need to think about your goals. You need to separate your goals out into two categories, short-term goals, and long-term goals. Then you need to prioritize your short-term goals to see which ones should come first in the series. This will help you pick the starting five needed to get you to your first goal.

Remember that every season of your life will be different. Therefore, you will use a slightly altered starting five for each goal. Considering an actual basketball team, many things can happen in the middle of a season. Players can get hurt which takes them out for a few games or a full season. Players can even get traded in the middle of the season with little to no notice. A coach has to be ready to come up with a new winning strategy moving forward. Similar to your season in life, things may change. Your goals may shift for one reason or another, but you need to effectively look at your human resources to discern what players will be the best choice for your starting five.

Having a starting five in networking is great because you need a team of people in your corner. The average NBA basketball team has around 14 players on their roster. At least 8 of those players must suit up for every game. So, while five players may start the game, there are at least 3 other players who are waiting for the coach to find the right time to put them into play. It's important to have these players suited up and ready to go at a moment's notice because you never know when you may need them. As the coach of your season, you need to be ready to use the right players at the right time to help you achieve your goals.

Here are some example seasons you will be in during your time in college and some potential starting five players you could use.

- Internship season (Freshman/Sophomore yr) – Academic Advisor, Faculty Advisor, Instructor/Professor, Work Supervisor, and Career Advisor
- Graduate school season (Sophomore/Junior yr) – Faculty Advisor x 2, Site Supervisor from the internship, Program Coordinator and Career Advisor
- Career season (Senior/Graduate School) – Faculty Advisor, Site Supervisor x 2, Career Advisor, Informational Interview contact

Let me explain to you how important a starting five is when you are trying to achieve a goal like getting an internship or landing a job. When I was looking for a job while I was finishing my master's degree, I had a team of people who were working for *me* and forwarding me job postings or potential job openings within our line of work. These people were all individuals I met through networking. They were the individuals I put in my starting five. They knew who I was as a student and a professional, which meant they would vouch for me. The minute that a job opportunity popped up on their email, came across their desk in a memo or was mentioned at a meeting, they immediately contacted me about it. Sometimes I would receive 3 to 5 emails from the players in my starting five about the same opportunity!

As the coach of my starting five, if I showed interest in the opportunity, they would immediately email or call about the position to find out more information on my behalf. They would also drop my name to let the hiring manager know I would apply for that position soon. They would sing my praises of how I was an awesome person, a hard worker and the ultimate professional. This is one of those instances where you can't really brag on yourself. It's better to let other people do the bragging for you. My starting five was willing and able to put in a good word for me, which put me on the hiring manager's radar when looking for qualified candidates. A good word can go a long way. Having a trusted person on the inside to vouch for you is incredibly important. THIS IS THE #1 WAY TO GET A JOB! This is how the real world works. Now that you know the rules of the game, you can come up with a great starting five to help you win. You will work when your starting five works for you.

• • •

Remember that graduate school interview that I mentioned before? The one where they grilled me on the experience memo that I had missed? Well, I was also crumbling under the pressure from another heap of questions on the "networking" memo that I had unintentionally missed.

I was getting pulverized with questions about networking during my graduate school interview. The program coordinator of the graduate program I was trying to get into was hammering me with questions I didn't think I had to answer at this point. *Do you know anyone in the field? Have you done any internships or experience within the field? Do you have any family or friends within the school district?* After answering a resounding "no" to every question she asked me, she finally levelled me with her final question on the subject. *How do you expect to get a job?* I thought the question was one of the most bizarre questions I had ever heard. Fumbling for an answer, I stammered, "Well, I hoped that the connections I made during my two-year graduate program would open job opportunities for me." The program director just looked at me... puzzled. The silence in that room was deafening. *Oh, no... did I miss a memo?* I had. A BIG ONE. I assumed that getting the degree would get me the job. I didn't realize that there was more to it than that.

Soon, I would get the memo. Jobs are found through networking and making professional connections. I can see now that the program director was trying to make me understand that jobs didn't materialize just because I had a degree. If I were to get a job after graduation, I would have to be intentional about my time while I was in school. I made it my mission to connect with as many professionals within the field as I could. During the final year of my graduate program, I conducted over 30 informational interviews. *I was an informational interview machine.* I was making connections with professionals at every university and college, 4-year and 2-year school, public and private institution within an hour radius of my home and then some. Once I found out the power of the informational interview, there was no stopping me.

To be honest, not every informational interview led to a profound insight or a key professional connection. There were times when I walked out of the meeting confused, frustrated and even disappointed. *I would NEVER want to work there. That person sucked. That sounds like a horrible job. There's no way I would get paid enough to put up with all that.* But you know what was awesome about that bad stuff? A bad informational interview just allowed me to close a door. Closed doors are good when you are trying to narrow the path to your goal. Sometimes it takes a few closed doors to find the right door to walk through.

The good informational interviews led to some fantastic connections I still have to this day. All of my internships and job offers to this point have been because of my informational interviews, the connections I made during those meetings. I can't stress enough to students how important networking and professional connections are to achieve your educational and career goals. It's a small world, and people know people. The more connections you make, the better of a chance you have to attain your goal. Use your time wisely by making professional connections early and often. Remember, you gotta network to get work.

Keep in mind, an informational interview is exactly what it sounds like. It is not a *job* interview where you are seeking a *job*. An *informational* interview is an interview where you are seeking *information* like a reporter investigating a story. You can find out just about anything during an informational interview. If there is a company you have dreamed of working for since you were a little kid, you can do informational interviews with individuals who already work at that company to find out how they got hired. You can find out about a job position, a title or a field of work through informational interviews. One of the best ways to learn about how to get somewhere is by asking someone who has already made it.

Okay, let's break this down. Imagine that you've always wanted to work for the FBI. Your first thought is: "How do I get a job with the FBI?" You could Google it. I'm sure there are tons of sites out there to let you know what you'll have to do to catch the eye of the FBI. Or you could have an informational interview with someone that works for the FBI. This individual could give you first-hand information of how they landed the job. Not only would this person be pulling back the curtain on all the secrets that the websites don't tell you, but they will also be more apt to tell you the mistakes they made in trying to get hired. People love bragging on themselves, and they also love giving advice. *Do it this way. Don't do it that way. If I had to do it all over again, I would do it like this. If I had known then what I know now, I would have done it like that.* It's truly amazing what people will tell you during an informational interview.

Informational interviews are unbelievably beneficial

because you are not only getting *information* from this particular person; you are *making a connection* on the inside. Now, someone on the inside *knows* you. They know you are a passionate professional with good intentions, hungry to know more about the field. They will also be more willing to give you names of other people you could meet with to conduct more informational interviews. This level of field research is invaluable when creating your network. If the connection is good, this person could be in your "starting five" when the season is right.

Making a good connection through informational interviews could lead to rare opportunities. The connection you made with the person who works for the FBI will now be more likely to think of you if an opportunity comes across their desk. *What kind of opportunity you ask?* Possibly job shadowing. Now that this person knows you are not a total fool and can conduct yourself like a professional, this person might be more willing to allow you to hang out with them for a day to get a better understanding of the job. This could lead to an internship, which could eventually lead to a job. Of course, this is a best-case scenario. Not every informational interview will be a door to more opportunities, but there is always the possibility of making a connection that could lead you closer to your ultimate goal.

I know what you are thinking. *This information is so incredibly helpful, but how do I find people for informational interviews?* That's a great question and thanks for the compliment. I'll tell you how to find the people. You simply have to ask. Ask your faculty advisors. Ask your site supervisor at your internship. Ask the instructors in your courses. You can even create a LinkedIn account and do what I call "professional creeping." (If you don't have a LinkedIn account, get one! You'll need it. It's like Facebook wearing a suit.) All you have to do with a LinkedIn account is type in the name of a position, company or career field into the search box and it will give you a laundry list of different people who fit into that category. Find a few people you are interested in and send them a message. It's as simple as that. Don't be afraid to reach out.

Let's do an on-the-spot example, shall we? Let's say that you want to work in Human Resources someday. Ultimately, you could see yourself as an HR Director. Wouldn't it be nice to have an informational interview with someone like that? I just went to my LinkedIn account and typed in "HR Director" in the search bar at the top of the page. That search gave me 1,893,616 results. *Okay... that is Crazy Town!* So, we'll need to narrow it down. You can filter down the search results by picking a location near you. I selected the Cleveland/Akron, Ohio area option. That narrowed my search to 6,154 results, which is still ridiculous.

You can narrow the search even more by filtering by companies of interest. However, in this example, I'm going to narrow down this search by applying another tactic that has worked for me in the past. I simply filter the search by schools. If I can find an alumnus from my school, then I might have a greater opportunity of them being more receptive to the idea of an informational interview. I graduated with my bachelor's degree from Marshall University in Huntington, West Virginia. Let's just see if I get anyone...? *BINGO!* I got 3 results. That is a more manageable number. If I wanted to really meet with them, I would then reach out to them in an effort to set up an informational interview.

With as many people as I contacted, I never once received a "no." I had a few individuals not reply, but that was definitely not the norm. Most people love talking about themselves. These little informational interviews provide individuals with a brief break in the day to do something out of the ordinary. Just reach out to people. You will see.

• • •

Every day I encounter a student who has yet to embrace the concept of networking. Take Molly for example. Molly was a bright student and was making great grades in school. She had aspirations of continuing on to get a graduate degree. She said she wanted to get her master's degree in school psychology. I asked Molly what kind of research she had done on school psychology. She said she looked on the internet. However, she couldn't give me real specifics on the career field. I asked her if she knew anyone that was working within the field as a school psychologist. She said no. I asked Molly if she had ever reached out to anyone to make professional connections within the field. She said no. I asked if she had talked to any faculty members to learn more about school psychology. Again, she said no. I asked her questions like, "How do you know you will like school psychology?" "Are there jobs out there for school psychologist?" "What is the job forecast for the school psychology field?" "What is required to be a school psychologist in your state?" "Are you planning to relocate?" Hearing Molly's lack of research reminded me of my lack of research prior to my graduate school interview. I was going in unprepared for the reality of what was awaiting me.

Getting through college can be tricky. Finding an internship and landing a job will be challenging too. Why do it alone? You can recruit a team of people that want to see you succeed. It takes some planning and strategy on your part, but the effort is worth it when the team you hand-picked helps you to reach those goals. As hokey as it may sound, truer words have never been spoken.

Teamwork makes the dream work.

Now that you have the educational foundation, the experience and your starting five in place, what do you do with all of this information? If only there was an office completely devoted to helping you neatly package all of this information so that you can use it to hit the ground running in the job search process. Oh wait! There is such an office. I guess you'll just have to keep reading to find out where this magical place is and how you can access it.

One Page Memo – Networking

Networking: That's like for old people, right? WRONG!

Who, What, When, Where, Why and How on Mastering this Memo

- **How?** Intentionally connect with individuals to form professional connections
- **What?** Conduct informational interviews with individuals within your desired career field for field research (Recruit for starting five)
- **When?** Early and often
- **Who?** Faculty Advisors, Instructors, Career Advisors, Informational interview contacts...etc.
- **Where?** Everywhere – school, work, internship...etc.
- **Why?** You're the coach and you need to create a starting five that will help you accomplish goals.

Your starting five will need to change depending on your season. That is why you need a team of people working for you to help you achieve your goals. Start recruitment for your team now and create a strong starting five:

- Be intentional
- Attend "networking" events
- Reach out to contacts
- Conduct informational interviews

YOUR MEMO - Networking

- First thing's first! Create a LinkedIn account!

- Find some connections through faculty and fellow students.

- What job/career field/company would you search? Write 3

- Who were your starting 5 getting into college?

- What is your next short-term goal?

- Who will be part of your starting 5 to accomplish that goal?

Aurora Alexander

MEMO NOTES

Memo #6

Career Services

"You give a poor man a fish, and you feed him for a day. You teach him to fish, and you give him an occupation that will feed him for a lifetime." –
Chinese Proverb

Do you like money? Would you like to eventually earn some money when you graduate from college? Is one of the main reasons you are attending college to someday receive a degree hoping you will get a good job to earn money? If you answered yes to any of these questions, Career Services will be your friend. This friend will be the liaison you need for anything that is job-related. Even if you are a freshman or sophomore, you still need Career Services. They will help you find internships and student employment opportunities and help you become a well-rounded professional. Get to know Career Services sooner rather than later. Be a frequent flyer. I mean, you're already paying for the services, you might as well put them to use.

• • •

You would never jump out of a plane without getting training and expertise from a skydiving instructor, would you? *This isn't Point Break*.[18] Even Tom Cruise went through training to jump out of an aircraft for Mission Impossible. If Tom Cruise wouldn't do it, then you shouldn't do it either. I don't know if that's a motto to live by, but it works in this scenario.

Think of career advisors as skydiving instructors. You go to a career advisor to receive help on how to neatly package your education, and your experience you've earned through internship, research and/or volunteer opportunities. Not only does your career advisor help you package that information, but they teach you how and when to pull the ripcords at the appropriate times. Once you are properly trained, the career advisor gets you up in the plane. That's when the career advisor gives you one last 'atta boy before you jump from the plane to free fall into the workforce.

Career advisors help smooth out your rough edges. Although you may feel that you have been navigating through school pretty seamlessly, there are things you must be equipped with before you enter the workforce that you won't learn in class. There is a huge transition from being a student and being a professional. It's a mind shift that a lot of students aren't prepared for when it happens. Employers don't want to hire students, they want to hire professionals. Even if you are looking for student employment opportunities and internships, people want to hire a professional, not a student.

Here is the mind shift. Students get away with murder in college. In college, you can show up late for a class or leave early. In fact, you can schedule a course and never show up for the entire semester. You'll get an F in the course, but you can still do it. You can miss exams and homework assignments. You can schedule makeup exams and earn extra credit to bring up your grade. You can go to tutoring, speak to the instructor and even sign up for services at the school to help you get through a class. You could also possibly receive an incomplete for a class (IN) if you cannot complete the required work due to extenuating circumstances. There are a lot of leniencies granted to students while in college.

In the workforce, however, employers are far less merciful. Students and people seem to forget about one simple thing about work. It's not about *you*, it's about the *job*. A person can easily be replaced. The harsh reality is that we are all easily replaced when it comes to a job. If I left my job today, there would be a hundred eager applicants chomping at the bit to fill this spot. It might be a little inconvenient for my coworkers for the brief period while they hired and trained a new person, but that would quickly fade. You do not get the same opportunities to earn extra credit with your employer. If you miss an important meeting, you look bad in the eyes of the employer. You may even lose your job. That's how the real world works. It's necessary for a student to learn these realities before it's too late.

The good news is that there is usually a team of individuals at your school that is dedicated to helping students realize the harsh realities of the workforce while teaching them how to become a more polished professional. Depending on your institution, they may call this office a variety of different names (Career Services, Career Exploration and Development, Career and Leadership Development Center... etc.) and the team of individuals that work there may have many titles. (Career Advisor, Career Counselor, Career Coach, Academic Program Officer, Internship Coordinator... etc.) Regardless of the titles, the intention is the same. The purpose behind these offices is for students to gain personalized attention through career advising, whether you are exploring majors and minors, or possible career options.

The services you will find at your institution's Career Services office will prove invaluable as you transition from college into the real world. The services may vary from office to office, but they cover the basics of what you will need to successfully navigate your career search. Some services may include:

- Major/minor exploration
- Career exploration
- Resume and Cover letter review
- Interview prep
- Mock interview

Some Career Services office even offer regular workshops and presentations geared toward professional development. Here are some topics that your institution may cover:

- Networking
- Workplace Etiquette
- Social Media
- Internship and Cooperative Education Opportunities
- LinkedIn Development
- Reference Development
- Career Fair Prep

Who's into free swag? EVERYONE! And nobody knows this more than Career Services. It's actually astonishing what some Career Services offices offer to students for free. I know that some offices offer a professional photograph which is necessary when creating professional online profiles and portfolios, otherwise known as "headshots." Other places will charge a pretty penny for such a photograph, but some Career Services offices offer these for free. Business cards can definitely be a costly purchase on a student's budget. Some offices can print business cards for networking purposes for free or at little cost, which can come in handy when conducting informational interviews. The institution where I work has a deal with a major department store where new suits for men and women are donated to students who meet the qualifications. This is perfect for students who need a professional outfit for interviews and other professional affairs. There are very few students who can afford to buy a $150-$200 outfit, not including tailoring.

I know what you are thinking at this point. *Could Career Services be any more awesome?* Oh yeah, they can! Not only is Career Services super convenient as a student, but you can also take advantage of their services as an alumnus. Most Career Services offices cater to alumni. Many experts believe that the average individual will change careers 5-7 times during their work life. Please, take a good look at that previous statement. The stat is about *careers*, not jobs. The average individual will have 5-7 brand new careers within their lifetime.

Maybe that statistic doesn't really make sense to you at this time of your life. I know that it didn't when I was in my bachelor's degree. *What's the difference between a job and a career? I thought that they were the same thing. Two different words, but pretty much the same meaning, right?* Wrong. A job is totally different than a career. A *job* is simply a way of earning money. You show up. You do your work. You get paid. The end. I've had plenty of jobs in my day. I was a lifeguard. I was a server. I folded sweaters at department stores. I was a cashier. J. O. B. S. I knew that there was no future with these employment opportunities. It was a means to an end. Plain and simple.

A *career*, on the other hand, is completely different. There is a future implied with the term "career." A career is where someone is dedicating a significant amount of time with their profession and/or education in order to make progress. The work that you do in your career will propel you forward by gaining responsibilities and experience. This propulsion is the exact fuel that you need in order to accomplish professional goals. Do you see the difference now? Jobs are stagnant. Careers have growth.

When taking another look at the above statistic, it might make a little more sense now. You will have plenty of jobs, but chances are that you will have a few different career shifts in your life, as well. There is a good possibility that you will have multiple jobs within a career field. This may seem a little confusing, but follow me. I currently work as an academic advisor and a career coach. Someday, I may have the title of career advisor or success coach or admissions counselor. Regardless of the title, I will probably continue to work in the counseling/advising career field. There are multiple job opportunities within a career field.

The above statistic is referring to actual career shifts. For this day and age, this is totally normal. Long gone are the days where you find a job after you graduate, work that same job for 40 years and then retire. Unfortunately, those days have gone the way of the dodo bird. Those days do not exist anymore. Companies close their doors, move overseas, get bought out, divisions merge, career fields evaporate and expand. There is no guarantee that the job you land after college will be around in 5-10 years. That's why you need Career Services. Plus, Career Services has kept their collective finger on the pulse, and they will tell you the latest trends of what employers want since the last time you were in the job market.

● ● ●

I met Jessica during one my many advising appointments. She was trying to get into graduate school. She was in her senior year of her bachelor's degree. Jessica was trying her best to finish strong while applying to graduate programs, which she found to be a time-consuming process. Jessica said she was frustrated because she didn't understand all the documents that were needed for the application process. Each graduate school had different requirements, and the process overwhelmed her. Resumes, cover letters, and personal statements were all documents that were needed, but she didn't know how to polish them enough to make them stand out to get noticed. Jessica also knew she would eventually interview for a graduate program. She was so nervous thinking about this because she said she had never been in an official interview before. I asked Jessica if she had ever visited the university's Career Services office. She said no. She didn't even realize that they could help her. She said she didn't realize that this office existed on campus. I could sympathize with her because I remember when I was trying desperately to get an internship.

Wow! I wish that we had one of those! I was referring to a Career Services office. I made this comment when I was trying desperately to get an internship with a Career Services office at another institution for my master's degree. I thought that this other institution was so rare and unique because it had an office completely devoted to helping students find jobs by helping them with resumes, cover letters and interviewing skills. *That's exactly what I need!* I remember thinking how advantageous it would be if my own university had a Career Services office to help me land the internship of my dreams.

I had made no real connections through

networking. *What's networking?* (I still hadn't gotten the memo at this point in my educational journey, but I was about to receive it. See Memo #5 on Networking if you have missed the memo too.) However, my faculty advisor mentioned that this might be a good opportunity for me. Plus, this internship was paid! That was unheard of in my area. There are some paid internships, but it is like finding a black cat in a coal cellar. In theory, they are there, but you'll probably never stumble across one. As luck would have it, I stumbled upon one. Another bonus for the internship was that it was in a field of work where I had shown interest, which was career advising. I had previously done a presentation on the area of career counseling because it had peaked my interest.

I knew this was the internship for me. I was determined to land the coveted spot. I spent the next two weeks creating the perfect resume. One week of that was during my summer vacation. While everyone was out at the beach having a fantastic time, I was indoors pacing the room trying to cultivate this amazing document to wow the director at the internship site. I spent hours getting opinions from different people, sorting through their feedback and reading articles online. My life was consumed with writing this resume. I had to make the perfect resume, or else I wouldn't get the internship. *If I didn't get the internship, then I wouldn't get the internship credit I needed to graduate. If I didn't graduate, I wouldn't be able to get a job. If I didn't get a job, how would I pay back my student loans?* I began to slowly unravel. This whole process was making me lose my mind.

```
All work and no play makes Aurora a dull girl.
All work and no play makes Aurora a dull girl.
All work and no play makes Aurora a dull girl.
All work and no play makes Aurora a dull girl.
All work and no play makes Aurora a dull girl.
```

Needless to say, I had become obsessed with this internship and the concept of a Career Services office. *Why don't we have one of those!? I'm a student too! I would enjoy a bit of career advising RIGHT NOW!* I remember expressing my frustration out loud during one of my classes. My friend Clay looked over at me in bewilderment and said, "Ya know, we got one of those too. Why don't you go to *our* Career Services office here at the school?"

I couldn't believe my ears. This office exists? On my campus? It's free? The fees of the office were already included in my tuition, but I didn't realize that. *And I'm just now finding out about this? How could this be?* I remember walking around in a state of utter confusion for the next few days. My mind was busy running through all the other institutions I had attended. *Did they have Career Services offices too that I didn't know about?* A quick search on the internet proved that they, in fact, did. I couldn't believe that all the time I had spent in my bachelor's degree and all the jobs I had held over the years, I had an unused Career Services office within my grasp. I never knew! As unfortunate as that thought was, I knew I couldn't change the past. The old Aurora could never use Career Services in those past memories, but I knew I could use them now. I wasted no time in doing that.

During all of this, as luck would have it, I ended up getting an interview for the internship. I had submitted the resume I had worked tirelessly on, and the site supervisor was interested.

Once I discovered I had access to my Career Services office at my university, I immediately made an appointment to meet with a career advisor. I could pick the reason for the appointment. Considering that my interview was on Tuesday, I made a mock interview appointment with my career advisor on Monday. I thought this mock interview would give me a chance to iron out any kinks before the real interview the next day.

Even though I was frustrated over the resume writing part of this process, I knew I had this interview in the bag. As I mentioned before in a previous memo, I thought I was pretty good at interviewing. I'm a funny and charming individual that has a passion for student success. *How could I possibly go wrong?* This mock interview was just a preliminary thing to stroke my ego. I wanted a professional from the career field to confirm how awesome I was by further solidifying my feelings. However, the mock interview didn't go quite as I planned.

The career advisor sat me down in his office and asked me questions as if it were the real interview. I quickly realized that I was out of my depth. I was not prepared to answer any of the questions he was hurling in my direction, and I was sinking fast. I think I'm good at BS-ing, but there was no BS-ing these questions. This was one of the first times I can ever remember truly being at a loss for words. Like a deer in headlights, I froze and stopped talking. Tears welled up in my eyes. My demeanor completely changed. The once confident and out-spoken candidate that originally sat down at the beginning of the interview was now just a shrunken heap who could barely catch her breath.

It was so excruciatingly bad that the career advisor stopped the interview. I couldn't have been more mortified. I had stories of individuals who had experienced spontaneous human combustion. I never really understood the concept but found it oddly fascinating. However, I could totally see something like that happening in this kind of situation. I was so embarrassed that I felt like my ears would catch on fire in the middle of the interview. At that point, I would have been thankful for spontaneous human combustion because there would have been a decent answer as to why I performed so horribly during the interview. *Why didn't I get the internship? Oh! It's because I burst into flames during the interview.* That sounded like an easier answer to swallow than the real reason. *Maybe I'm not as awesome as I think I am?*

Luckily, the career advisor had a heart. He saw that I was beating myself up pretty badly over my poor performance. He spent the rest of the appointment showing me where I went wrong and how to properly prepare for my big interview the next day. I was super thankful that I had made this appointment. I'm glad I made a fool of myself in front of my career advisor and not in front of the Director of Career Services during my interview. Although I walked out of that appointment deflated, there was still hope.

I was down, but I wasn't out. I would not let that opportunity slip through my hands without a fight. I wanted this internship so bad I could taste it. Not only would I be getting the credit I needed for graduation and the experience I needed to get a job, but I would also get paid for it. I knew that paid internships were as scarce as hen's teeth. Now, I had the tools I needed to nail that interview. And, I knew how to use them, thanks to Career Services.

I know that you're probably dying to know whether I got the internship, right? Well, I did! I knocked the interview out of the park. *Booyah!* (Not bragging, just proud of myself.) That was a massive hurdle I was unprepared to jump over. However, I cleared the jump because I used the resources offered through Career Services. What I learned through that experience will stick with me for a lifetime. My career advisor didn't just give me a fish. He *taught* me *how* to fish. I couldn't be more thankful.

The world's expectation of you as a college student is that you pop out the other side of your higher education experience as a polished professional. However, becoming a polished professional doesn't happen by accident. There's more to getting a job than just having good grades or a degree. For example, employers desire a potential candidate who is the perfect puzzle piece to the specific job position. This is not about you, it's about your fit. Helping students understand how to prove their professional fit to potential employers is the ultimate goal of the Career Services office. The trends, tips, and techniques you will learn through Career Services will help build the professional foundation needed for you to successfully hit the ground running in today's workforce.

Now that you have some idea of how to effectively jump the next set of hurdles, whether it is getting into a graduate program or finding a job after your bachelor's degree, you need to start thinking about the consequences of those actions. Making the decision to either get a job or go on for more education will inevitably have an impact on your wallet. It's important for you to at least start thinking about your finances before it hits you in the face.

One Page Memo – Career Services

Career Services: I don't need it until I want a job, right? WRONG!

Who, What, When, Where, Why and How on Mastering this Memo

- **How?** Google your institution's name and career services
- **What?** See what comes up for your institution
- **When?** Office hours, services, events, and workshops
- **Who?** Name of contact person (Coordinator/Advisor) and/or contact information (email and phone)
- **Where?** Office location and location of upcoming events
- **Why?** You want to make money someday, right?

The things that you will learn through career services will help build the professional foundation needed for you to succeed in today's workforce.

Contact your college's Career Services Office to find out about:

- Available services Fairs
- Online resources
- Alumni connections

- Career and Internship
- Programs and workshops
- Career aptitude tests

YOUR MEMO – Career Services

- Where is your Career Services office on campus?

- What is the contact information?

- Hours of operation?

- What services do they offer?

- What services could you use to accomplish your short-term goals?

- What services could you use to accomplish your long-term goals?

- Do they offer any workshops that you could attend?

Aurora Alexander

MEMO NOTES

M e m o   # 7

Finances

"Money is the opposite of the weather. Nobody talks about it, but everybody does something about it." –
Rebecca Johnson

I'm not a financial planner. I don't even play one on TV. I am not claiming to be a financial expert by any stretch of the imagination. But, as Sir Arthur Conan Doyle said, "It is easy to be wise after the event."[14] I can definitely look back now and see where I made mistakes and where I could have maximized my opportunities rather than squandered them. This memo will not be a deep dive into the world of personal finances or financial aid. However, I will try to provide broad tips for you to adopt on your educational journey now that will prove beneficial in the long run. At this point, you need to understand that the decisions that you make for your future have financial consequences. Scholarships vs. Student loans. Or 2-year-degree vs. 4-year-degree. Public vs. private. Working full-time vs. part-time. Living on-campus or off-campus. All of these decisions make an impact on your future. You need to know your options moving forward.

Who wants to work until dirt is shoveled over their grave? Not me! But I probably will because I have not properly saved for retirement. I had plenty of time to save. I was a young adult at 18, 19, 20, and 21-years-old. *Save for retirement? That's crazy talk. I just got started!* I was working little random jobs here and there as a server, a sales associate and a pearl diver. The thought of saving for retirement while working these jobs was utterly ridiculous.

I wasn't completely against the thought of saving money. I had a savings account. Unfortunately, it was basically just a secondary checking account for me. I was always making withdraws or transferring money over from my checking to make ends meet. I thought I would do my *real* savings when I got a *real* job. I didn't really equate my various part-time jobs as *real* work. Those positions were always temporary in my eyes. So, in the meantime, I would just spend whatever I made and worry about saving later.

There were things I failed to take into consideration. First, I knew I wasn't making big dollars at these little jobs, which made me dismiss the money I made. I thought when I got my degree, and I got my *real* job, I would then rake in cash. Here's the thing... money is money, whether you make it by flipping burgers or crunching numbers at an accounting firm. It's just as green and has the same money smell. Saving doesn't have to wait.

Another thing I failed to realize was the level of responsibilities I would have once I had my degree and how little I would have to put into my savings then. By the time I got out of school and got my job, I had a ton of bills and responsibilities that were taking priority over my saving habits. I had to worry about student loans, a mortgage, health insurance, and my family. I realized that life doesn't get any easier as you progress. In fact, it gets increasingly trickier to successfully pull off the delicate balancing act of work, family and personal responsibilities.

• • •

Have you ever seen a plate spinning act on a late-night talk show? When I was growing up in the 80s, they would have some sap on the show who, as an act, would spin plates. I was never too impressed with these individuals. I don't think the rest of America was either, because they would sandwich these performers between two well-known guests. This plate spinner was just a circus act that was used as a filler. I guess I had a sick sense of humor as a kid because I was always secretly rooting for one (or more) of those plates to fall and smash on the ground. However, as an adult, I have a deep appreciation for the art of plate spinning.

If you are feeling squirrelly, look up "Erich Brenn Plate Spinning on *The Ed Sullivan Show*." It is a short clip that lasts a little over three minutes, and it will give you an idea of what I'm talking about with this analogy. Just to warn you, the first minute and a half will be boring. I know what I thought when I first saw it. *I could not be more bored.* However, about 1:45 into the clip, I got into it. *This cat has skills.* Slowly but surely, the plate spinner will win you over because he is master of prioritization. It's amazing, actually. Now, I see the skill it takes to do this kind of activity I could never fully appreciate when I was a kid.

NEWS FLASH... THIS JUST IN! As an adult, that is all life is... spinning plates. Slowly but surely, you will gain more responsibilities. You'll get an apartment or buy a house. You may get married and then start a family. You buy a car or two. You'll have health insurance and car insurance. Before you know it, you'll have a stack of bills piling up on your kitchen table or in your inbox. You will go on vacation if you're lucky. Plus, you must plan for Christmas and holidays, as well as birthdays and anniversaries. I'm not even mentioning the occasional emergencies that pop up. You might need a root canal, or you need a new set of tires. There may be a big storm that comes through your neighborhood that causes raw sewage to back-up in your basement, and you have to call a plumber on a holiday weekend to fix the problem. *I'm sour about that last one because it JUST happened to me!* Spinning plates... that's all it is. It's a perfectly strategic balancing act that requires a cool head and a mountain of anticipation.

• • •

Zachary came into my office and was very uncertain about his future. He had a ton of questions about what he should or shouldn't do moving forward with his bachelor's degree. He was progressing pretty well in his degree program and could graduate early. He asked if this was a good idea. I told him it all depends on his future plans. I said the best thing to do in this situation is to really weigh out the pros and cons of finishing early. He said if he waited to graduate, he would have to sign a new lease. Although, he was considering possibly finishing his degree online. He said he was applying to graduate school, but most of the programs didn't start until the following fall. If he graduated early, this meant that he would have 8-9 months before his program would start. What would he do in the meantime? Would he continue to work in fast food or would he need to find a job within his field? Which would look better for him moving forward? He wanted to save money before he started graduate school, but he didn't know which choice would be best. I understood his frustration because I had a hard time discerning what would be the best decision for me financially.

At this point in the memo, I will take a "fearless moral inventory" of my finance wins and losses from when I was in college. I made a lot of mistakes, but I also made some mediocre decisions. Although the mediocre decisions weren't necessarily bad, they weren't amazing either. What I failed to realize with my finances in all of this was to make intentional decisions to set myself up for success in the long run, not to just merely scrape-by for the rest of my entire adult life. I will spend the rest of this memo discussing my top 3 wins/losses in my finances.

Financial Aid. The term "Financial Aid" can send shivers down a student's spine. The thought of filling out a FAFSA form can bring a lump to an incoming freshman's throat. I remember slowly tensing up when I realized that the deadline was approaching. It was such an overwhelming process back then. I know that technology has improved a lot of things over the years but seeking financial aid can still provoke fear in some students.

The first big mistake I made was thinking that financial aid was free money. I *knew* it wasn't free money. I signed promissory notes. I knew I would eventually pay this money back to the federal government. But for some reason, it never really seemed real. Because of my extended time in school, the loans didn't seem as imminent. Paying my school loans seemed like something I would *eventually* have to do, like dying. Eventually, I know that I will die. I didn't plan on that happening anytime soon, but I knew it was a reality. So, I put paying off my school loans in the same mental file folder as taking a dirt nap and forgot about it. I didn't realize how soon "someday" would turn into "today."

Another big mistake I made with financial aid was thinking that the Financial Aid Office could help me with my finances. I mean, the word "financial" is in the title. Why wouldn't they be able to help me with my finances, right? Wrong. The individuals that work in the Financial Aid Office are not financial planners. They will not talk to you about different mutual funds and stock options or be able to tell you the best rate you can get on a CD (certificate of deposit). These financial aid officers are more like interpreters of policies. If you have a question about how your financial aid award is determined or when will you receive financial aid, or what happens to your financial aid if you need to exit in the middle of a semester, Financial Aid can help you out with that. For information on managing your finances, you must speak with the appropriate professional.

Some colleges may offer something like a Financial Wellness service. The information is meant to educate students to create confident and financially independent individuals in society. These are only educational services, and they are not intended to act as a substitution for a consultation with a financial expert. Just remember, that the financial aid advisor can only answer questions about financial aid. *Makes sense, right?* Be mindful of their time and be clear with your questions because there is a line of 50 other students behind you that are waiting to inquire about their financial aid status. I just want you as a student to know of the scope of information that is covered through a financial aid office and where their knowledge ends.

A very common mistake for students, which I was no exception, is the student loan refund. What do you do with this money? There may be a time where you must withdraw from a class in the middle of the semester, which could prompt a refund check. Or maybe after all the tuition, books, boarding and food was paid, you had a little loan money left over. Even though I knew this was a refund of money, I would eventually have to pay back, at the moment, it felt like *bonus cash*!

Have you ever pulled out a coat from the back of your closet you haven't worn in a year or so only to find $20 in the pocket? That's a great feeling, isn't it? It feels like bonus cash, but I know that the money is mine, to begin with. In fact, I was probably at some point looking for that $20 back when I misplaced it. No matter. It's in my sweet little hand right now. The same feeling surged through me when I got a refund check. *Jackpot! Bonus cash! It's going to be a good day!* No matter the circumstances, my bank account was now a little fuller.

At this point, I had a choice. *What should I do with this money?* Give it back? *Yeah right.* Save it for a rainy day? *Have we met? I don't think so.* I parlayed that money into a few things. I didn't take advantage of a study abroad program, but I used the money from a student loan refund to finance a trip I took to Europe with my best friend, Krista. Not necessarily the best deal because I wasn't really factoring in the interest portion of the loan. I am still paying back that European excursion. I also took a refund and purchased a laptop, but not just ANY laptop. I'm talking the best of the best. I got a laptop with all the bells and whistles. It was top of the line, and it had the best guarantee money could buy. That laptop would power me to get through the rest of my bachelor's degree and help me finish my master's degree. The good news is that I still have that laptop and use it every day. *I really bought a great laptop.* The bad news is that I'm still paying for that baby because of the interest. So, was it a smart move in the end? Not really, but I'm well aware of my mistakes now.

What should I have done in this scenario? What should you do if you are ever in this scenario? You have two options. Option one, give the money back. Most schools will return the money for you if you provide a written request for cancellation between 30 to 120 days from the disbursement day of your loan. If your school does not process the cancellation request, it will be up to you to contact the loan servicer directly. If you miss the 120-day deadline, you can still give the money back, but it will be submitted as a payment. Simply send the leftover money to your student loan servicer as you would any other loan payment. You will still be required to pay fees or any accumulated interest, but it will not be nearly as steep as if you waited years to repay. It could save you hundreds, if not thousands of dollars in the long run.

The other option if you were to receive refund money from student loans is to keep it strictly for emergencies. I mean *REAL* emergencies. I'm talking like a loved one dies in a tragic shark attack while scuba diving on the Great Barrier Reef and you are the only individual in the family that can go claim the body in order to bring it back home to the United States. You will need a last-minute plane ticket to Australia, which could run you anywhere from $2,000-$3,000. *That* kind of emergency. Last-minute weekend trip to Vegas with your friends does not qualify as an emergency in this scenario. See the difference? Even though some people may discourage you from saving this money and suggest that you pay it back immediately because of the accrued interest, sometimes it just feels better to have a chunk of money set aside just in case. Do not spend your student loan refund on things like furniture, new clothes, a new car, a vacation or alcohol. *Yeah, yeah, yeah...* I know that I spent my student loan refund on a trip to Europe, but I am STILL paying for that trip. If I had known then what I know now, I would have gone to Europe through a Study Abroad program where I would have qualified for scholarships that would have partially paid for my entire trip, if not entirely. Shoulda, woulda, coulda, right?

● ● ●

SAVINGS. Speaking of having a chunk of money set aside, I will talk about my mistake with savings accounts. I remember when I created a savings account I thought I had really made it. *Look, Mom! I'm adulting!* Unprompted, I walked into my local bank and created a savings account because that's what adults do, right? I thought since I'm in college, pay bills and work I should have a savings account to stash some money away for safe-keeping. Mind you, I was working as a server and never received a paycheck. Therefore, I rarely made a point to go to the bank because I always had cash. So, guess who deposited no cash into her savings? *This cat right here!* This meant that I had little to no savings in my savings account.

Another mistake with my savings came when I did finally get a job that had a paycheck. I would deposit a majority of my money into my checking account, and I would always leave myself a little cash. Then the money I would put into my savings was just a sliver of a percentage of my check. The effort I was making with my savings was merely an afterthought. How much can you truly save if you are in that mind frame?

I was looking at my savings through the wrong lens. Financial guru, Dave Ramsey says, "Saving must become a priority, not just a thought. Pay yourself first."[15] I never thought of putting money into my savings as *paying myself.* Looking at my savings from this angle gives me a totally different perspective on the concept. In college, I would deposit $20 here and $50 there. I didn't look at my savings as a payment to myself or investment in my future, I looked at it as though I was depriving myself of something. In my mind, it was like a punishment. I looked at the money I was saving as a night out with my friends I wasn't having or a new outfit I wasn't buying. Putting the money in this account was like a penalty, a financial hand-slap. *I could go to movies if it wasn't for my savings.* My savings account was holding me back! *I would be out having the time of my life if it wasn't for my savings.*

Over time, I began to unconsciously harbor negative feelings towards my savings account. It was like my personal financial judge. The low balance of my savings staring back at me made me feel guilty because I wasn't depositing enough. The balance was so low it was virtually useless. *This isn't a savings account. This is a joke.* What's the point of having a savings account if there is no real balance to help me out when I need it? I needed to get serious about my savings if I ever wanted to have a better financial relationship with this account.

I started saving. I made an intentional effort to put money into my account. I stayed consistent and made myself contribute a minimal amount from every check. Before long, the balance was rising. I was quite proud of myself. *Look at me, Mom! I have a balance!* I saw the world differently. I would look at the price of something and mentally sum it up. *I could buy that if I wanted. I could go on that trip if I wanted. I have the money for it. I'm an adult, and I have saved.* Then one day, I saw something I wanted, and it was a big-ticket item. It was a trip to New York City. I had been before, but this was different. This was a specific package that included many bells and whistles. I wanted to go, and I had the money. So, I went! It felt great to do something with the money I had saved. *Now, THIS is being an adult!*

I realized that if I consistently saved a little, I could then afford bigger things and I did just that. Except, my savings was now turning into a secondary checking out for bigger purchases. I would save for a little while only to drain it as soon as I saw something else. Again, I was missing the point of a savings account. I could never save more than $500-$700. I would always see something and buy it before I could break a grand in the bank. I could not see past a few months in the future. I only lived in the *now.* Looking back, if I had only stayed consistent with my savings and not drained it every two to three months, I would have pretty nice sized nest egg today. How was I to know one day I wouldn't be 21 and I might get to the ripe old age of 36? *Who am I, Miss Cleo?* (YouTube that 90s flashback.)

CREDIT CARDS. My final big mistake was with credit cards. And yes, this is the dreaded credit card talk. As a warning, you won't be able to swing a dead cat by the tail without hitting someone pushing a credit card on you as you walk on a college campus. And they ALWAYS have free swag, t-shirts, sunglasses, bags, pens and free tickets to events. They would probably give away their firstborn to you if they knew you would open a line of credit. They try to sell them by saying you get "cash back" and it raises your credit score. They plant the seeds now of increasing your credit score, so you will be able to qualify for a nice house when you graduate with your degree. Makes total sense, right? It did to me.

Up until their divorce when I was sixteen, my parents had excellent credit. Even as a teenager, I was well aware of their financial success. They told me how important it was to have a good credit rating and how I would need that as I navigated through adulthood. *Oh! So, this is how I get started? Awesome.* I thought I would just buy certain things on my card and pay off the balance of the monthly statement. I thought this concept was so simple. I wondered how people would ever get in trouble with credit cards. *I will only buy things I have money for at this moment. Why would I buy something if I know that I don't actually have the money for it?* I thought I was SO smart.

I was able to keep up my brilliant "paying-off-the-balance" plan for a couple of months. Then I made my first mistake. I drained my bank account because of an "emergency." Mind you, this emergency was getting my video entry to the producers of the Real World: Back to New York (That's right. The reality show.) before the deadline. At 18, I really didn't possess the discernment necessary to distinguish between a real emergency versus a need, versus a want. To submit the application, I *needed* to submit a videotape. (Remember those? Google it!) I *needed* to buy a blank tape. ($) I *needed* to send it in the mail ($) overnight ($) for it to get there on time. Within a week, I received notice I had moved on to the next round. At that point, I *needed* to overnight ($) the 16-page application back to their office in California. Then, they wanted to set up a video/phone call with me for an interview. I couldn't possibly wear any clothing I already owned. I *needed* to run out immediately to buy a new outfit ($). After my casting interview, I *needed* to overnight ($) my videotape of the interview to the producers. As you can see, these things clearly fell into the "emergency" category because time was of the essence. This is Hollywood, people. Time waits for no star! (eye roll)

I remember looking at my mom during all of this and complaining about my finances. I told her I had drained my bank account with all of these *needs* for The Real World casting process and I was forced to buy my everyday necessities with my credit card, like gas, food and stuff for school. My mom looked at me with a sneer and said, "Who's fault is that?" *My mom is totally oblivious. She truly doesn't understand THE REAL WORLD.* (As a side note, I made it to the top 20 finalists for that season of The Real World. So, my "emergency" really didn't pan out how I had wanted.) With these little purchases, I opened a door I could never shut.

The first couple of times I used my credit card for miscellaneous purposes, I felt like a complete tool. *Yes, I am using a credit card for a pad of notebook paper and a pack of gum. Got a problem with that?* Then the internal judgment of how ridiculous my purchases were beginning to subside. I swiped my credit card everywhere they would accept it. Remember, all the while, I am slowly boosting my credit score. *I want to buy a house someday.* Swipe. *Soon I will buy a new car.* Swipe. *What's the big deal? I'm still paying off the balance every month.* Swipe. Swipe. Swipe. Before I knew it, I was really wearing out the magnetic strip on the back of my card.

My next mistake with my credit card might be my biggest. I began to no longer pay off my balance, but I opted for the minimum payment. *Why should I drain my bank account just to pay off my balance every month?* My rationale was that I would pay off the balance the next month. Unfortunately, the next month would come, and I would only pay the minimum. I was continuing to use my credit card, but I was still only paying the minimum. Things quickly escalated from there.

Looking back now, I had no rhyme or reason behind my spending and saving habits. It was a juggling act between my checking, savings and credit accounts. Pay this here. Put some money there. Pull the money back out and put it over here. I was robbing Peter to pay Paul only to turn around and rob Paul to pay Peter. It was crazy and made no sense in the long run. It was a horrible mess and I strongly discourage anyone from getting into a similar situation. No matter how benign the situation is with your personal credit cards, if left untreated, the balance can become cancerous in the long run.

• • •

Now that we have all had a big laugh over my financial blunders, here are the top 5 things you need to do concerning *your* finances in college.

1. Financial Aid and Student Loans–You should know what you are walking into and what is waiting for you on the other side of your degree. Be careful with refunds. This is not "bonus cash." You will have to pay this money back with interest. Again, are you responsible enough to carry the weight of the consequences associated with student loan debt?
2. Create a budget–The word "budget" is not a bad word. Think of it as a "grown-up

allowance." Determine your fixed expenses (rent, tuition, books, car payments, utilities, food... etc.) and your discretionary expenses (clothing and entertainment). Add those expenses together and subtract from your income. This may be hard to do if you do not track your purchases. There are reputable budgeting apps out there where you can sync your bank account to track your purchases.

3. Create a savings account–Pay yourself first! I know that you think you will live forever, but you most definitely will not. You will not always be in your 20s. Before you know it, you'll be 36-years-old and wonder where all the time went. If you start saving and make consistent deposits into your savings now, you will have the money for true financial emergencies and big expenses in life.

4. Live within your means–If you have created an effective budget and accounted for appropriate savings, living within your means should be the result. Considering you are in college, you will probably make next to no money. So, be prepared to make sacrifices when it comes to eating out or buying expensive technology.

5. Avoid accumulating consumer debt–Living outside your means will definitely lead to you accumulating consumer debt (credit cards, furniture, car, and other non-essentials). Strengthen the discernment of what is an emergency vs. urgency vs. luxury. Don't be afraid to question your choices. *Will I die if I do not buy this or take care of this situation?* If the answer is no, then it's probably not a legitimate emergency. Therefore, you don't *need* to put it on your credit card. Ultimately, know your limits. Are you responsible enough to carry the weight of the consequences associated with consumer debt?

Now that you have a firm grasp of the not-so-obvious

concerning your personal finances, you'll need to address your emotional health in school. Let's face it... finances can cause emotional drama. School is demanding, and life is challenging. Sometimes these entities can add up to this, Life + School = Emotional Instability. Emotional instability in school can lead to negative outcomes in your future. Poor grades and dropping out of school are just some of the outcomes that could impact your life because of depression or anxiety. Where do you turn for help in this area of life? I guess you'll just need to keep reading, won't you?

Aurora Alexander

One Page Memo – Finances

Finances: You mean like Financial Aid, right? WRONG!

Who, What, When, Where, Why and How on Mastering this Memo

- **How?** Actively save money and live within your means
- **What?** Budgeting your finances = Grown-up Allowance
- **When?** NOW!
- **Who?** Seek advice from experts to learn more (NOT Financial Aid)
- **Where?** Search the internet for credible resources
- **Why?** Sacrifice a little now to pay off big time later

Financial success stories from other people are actually years of sacrifice and consistent dedication of living on a budget. Start your success story today.

Be a real adult and follow these steps:

- Create a budget
- Utilize a savings account
- Live within your means
- Avoid consumer debt
- Understand student loans

YOUR MEMO – Finances

- Where is your Financial Aid office located?

- How much was the total amount of your college bill this semester?

- How much per class? Room and Board?

- Did you receive scholarships? If so, how much?

- Did you receive student loans?

- If yes to student loans, how much was offered vs. accepted?

- What is your interest rate?

MEMO NOTES

Memo #8

Counseling

"When self-care becomes a priority everything in your life gets a little easier." - Michelle Farris, LMFT

I always tell students that life happens during college. Let me take a minute to tell you a few of the challenging things I faced during my time in college in no particular order. Three of my grandparents died. I got married. I got divorced. A good friend committed suicide. I had a kid. I switched careers. I moved out of state. I got into a car accident. My car was totaled. (This left me with severe whiplash and months of physical therapy.) I could go on with more things that happened, but I will spare you.

Just for clarification, my time in school lasted a lot longer than the expected 4 years. Let's just do some simple math, shall we? *1 + 2...add the hiatus with that other one several years later... that's 5... then carry the 1... beep bop boop... equals (=) 14.* It took me <u>FOURTEEN</u> years to get my bachelor's degree. I want you to take a minute to let the deep unadulterated reality of that statement sink into your brain. *Fourteen years to finish a four-year degree.* To paraphrase one of my favorite movies, *Tommy Boy,* "shade over a decade" quote.[16] However, in my defense, it was not a continuous fourteen years of college. I took a significant hiatus or four within that fourteen years *because* of the substantial things that happened during my time in college.

If any one of these things happened to an individual, it would be expected that there would be a season of transition, which could prove to be difficult. With everything I mentioned that I experienced, I struggled. I struggled with severe depression and anxiety. It was hard for me to maintain consistency with some of these transitions. The expectations that come with taking college courses and performing well seemed virtually impossible. That is why I needed to take a break at certain points during my journey to restore homeostasis in my life, to find a *new* normal.

Over time, I would adjust to my *new* normal, and I would consider going back to school. Thanks to counseling, I could overcome these obstacles, good and bad. I believe that everybody would benefit from a dose of counseling at one point or another. However, it never dawned on me to seek counseling at my college campus. I didn't even know that was an option. It wasn't until after I graduated with my master's in counseling with an emphasis in higher education that I realized that there were counseling services on many college campuses. Sometimes these services are free! That would have helped me when I was a poor college student.

It's important to understand that maintaining a healthy mental and emotional well-being is vital in contributing to a student's success in college. There are hundreds of reasons why you would need to seek counseling to sustain positive mental health. There are plenty of resources at your fingertips that were created for someone just like you. Be mindful of using the counseling services that are most appropriate for you in your current situation. If you have questions about what resource would work best for you, all you need to do is ask.

● ● ●

April came in to see me for a required advising appointment. I knew she was relatively new to campus because she had just started a few months prior. I asked her how she was adjusting to college life and she said "okay," but it didn't seem convincing. April said her grandmother died the same weekend she moved into the dorms. She had to go back home, which meant that she missed the first week of courses. She's about 2 hours away from her mother and April said her mom was taking her grandmother's death pretty hard. I asked how April was adjusting to her *new* normal with the death and she said she was having a hard time juggling classes with the coursework. Plus, she said her mom was relying on her for emotional support, which was draining on April. April started crying. I asked her if she knew about the counseling services that were available to her on campus. She was puzzled by my question. "I could see a counselor here on campus?" I told her about the different resources available on campus and encouraged her to reach out. I reminded her it's not selfish to take care of herself. As I said those words, I remember someone saying the same thing to me when I was in college.

• • •

Maintain yourself like you maintain your car. I have always said you can tell how my personal life is going by the appearance of my car. Is it clean? Does it look like a garbage can on wheels? If it looks like a homeless person is living in my car, then I might need a bit of mental maintenance. Just like my car, I don't need to go in for mental maintenance every week. However, I will admit that sometimes I need to go in for some maintenance once a year or so. That's just the reality. Sometimes I'm under a tremendous amount of stress or a tragic event happens like the death of a loved one where I need some minor maintenance to adjust to my *new* normal. When I was younger, I ran my cars until the wheels fell off, literally. No maintenance EVER! My cars didn't last that long. Your mental health is very similar. In the words of American novelist, Tom Robbins, "There's birth, there's death, and in between there's maintenance."[17] Words to live by. Believe me, your brain and your car will thank me for it later.

I mentioned before that I struggled with severe depression and anxiety. In fact, depression and anxiety virtually crippled me when I was in my late teens and all throughout my 20s. I had two significant events happen within the same month that took place when I was 21 that only exacerbated my struggles. I broke up with my boyfriend of two years. I was truly devastated. It was a toxic relationship to begin with, and we both decided that it was best to end things to preserve our sanity. Even though it was for the best, it didn't make it feel any better.

To make matters worse, my dog (of 14 years) had to be put to sleep because of a stroke that same week. I could barely function. These seemingly common negative events that can happen to anyone had turned into major stressors for me. Not only was my heart broke, but it felt like it had been ripped out of my chest and set on fire. I had two major life events happen in the same week, and I was struggling to maintain sanity. To top it all off, this was August, and I was supposed to start school in a few days. *How in the world am I supposed to focus on class and making good grades?* The idea sounded so absurd. I had already taken a semester off before. I knew my mom expected me to keep going. My family had certain expectations of me. I couldn't bear the thought of disappointing my mom on top of everything else that I was going through.

Despite better judgment, I continued with school that semester. My depression was crippling. Depression, for me, was the inability to construct a future. I couldn't see past my nose. It was like living in a fog. I couldn't forecast what I was doing next week, let alone, next year. That created a level of anxiety in me that was suffocating. I felt as if I was drowning, but I was so paralyzed from depression I couldn't swim. Quality of life was something I didn't have much of at the time.

The repercussions of my depression and anxiety played out in every aspect of my life. I wasn't able to set appropriate goals for myself. I could not pick a major that was really suited to my skills and interests because I hated my life so much. Everything looked better than my life. That's one reason I believe television and movies had such a huge impact on my life. In my depressive stupor, I would lay and watch TV. The people on the screen seemed happy. *Hey! I want to be happy too.* So, as soon as I would get the energy, I would run right out and change my major. Now I realize that I was looking to cure my depression and anxiety by changing my circumstances rather than looking inward.

Now with my new major, I would enroll in new courses. I would try to set attainable goals with my study habits. *No matter how tired I am, I will make myself study at least 2 hours each night.* When it was time to study, I would bargain with myself. *I'm too tired. I will just double up on studying tomorrow night. I will devote 4 hours tomorrow.* Tomorrow would come and no studying. There were days I didn't even take a shower or brush my teeth because of depression. How was I supposed to have the energy and discipline to study or stay focused for hours upon end? I would set these goals and never attain them, which would only make me more depressed. I would do poorly in my courses because of my lack of studying, which again only made things worse. It was a vicious cycle I didn't know how to break.

I remembered hearing that people who worked out regularly struggled less with depression. I tried working out. I thought if I could make little goals of working out a little every day, I could overcome my depression. As you can imagine, I would make the same little goals for myself. *I will work out every day for an hour.* Nope. *I will work out 5 days a week.* Try again. *Okay... 3 days.* Fail. *I'll start next week.* Again, I was finding it challenging to keep my end of the bargain with a halfway decent hygiene routine. How was I expecting to dedicate myself to a new workout regime?

The chain reaction of my depression and anxiety trickled into my personal life too. Now that I didn't have a boyfriend, I had tons of free time, and I wanted to make new friends. Unfortunately, I was so physically and mentally drained from fighting with my depression I didn't have the energy to put into forging new relationships. The thought of making a friend sounded exhausting. The whole thing made me want to lie down and take a big ole nap. I spent my Friday and Saturday nights in my bed, in stinky old pajamas, watching Seinfeld and Frasier reruns. It was a sad state of affairs.

For some reason, I chose to power through school because I felt like it was something I *should* to do. Somehow, not going to class and never studying meant that my grades suffered that semester. *SHOCKER! Who would have ever guessed?* I took four classes that semester. I failed three of those courses. The only reason I didn't fail the fourth one was because I withdrew from it mid-semester. Clearly, I should have taken a break from school that semester, but I chose to keep up appearances by feebly cobbling together a *new* normal for myself. What's really sad is that I tried to do this alone.

Being that young, I had never really suffered losses like that before. This was the first time I was dealing with two great losses: a death and a break-up. I tried to rely on family and friends, but they really didn't know how to help me. They tried their best to cheer me up, but this situation needed something more than that. Being able to "turn my frown upside-down" would not cure this mind-numbing ache inside me. I was drowning, and I felt like no one could save me.

How would I overcome this? Going out? *Maybe.* Shopping? *Perhaps.* Alcohol? *Possibly.* All of these solutions were just temporary band-aids I tried to slap on to stop the hurt. What I needed was something to help me heal from the inside out. It felt like I tried everything under the sun to feel better, to get out of the fog, to swim to shore, to crawl out of the hole. My last resort was counseling. I finally reached the point where I had exhausted all other avenues. I couldn't fix this on my own. My support system wasn't helping. I felt I was too far gone. It was time to admit defeat and ask for help from a professional.

• • •

Although there were points that I took time off of school to regroup, and I forced myself to go to counseling, I was not consistent with my self-care. I am a giving person by nature. I would do anything for people to help them. However, I treat myself like I am the last person on the totem pole. I have never really been the person to place myself high on the list of priorities. I never looked at going to counseling as taking care of me. I found many excuses to not be consistent. *I don't have time. This is self-indulgent. This person or that person doesn't have to go to counseling, why do I? I shouldn't need this counseling stuff. I ought to function just fine without it.* These excuses for not being consistent seeped into my life and knocked me out of moving forward.

I looked at self-care as a burden. It took a long time to re-frame my perception of the concept of counseling. Instead of self-indulgence, it was actually self-preservation. Taking care of myself would allow me to take better care of others. *By being mentally and physically healthy, I will be able to help other people, which is what I really love to do.* Walking through life in a depressive fog knocked me out of doing the things I loved most in life. I was allowing this depression and anxiety to change me into someone I didn't like. It took me a long time to get to a healthy place. Now I can see that taking care of myself is not selfish. There is nothing wrong with taking care of me first in order for me to effectively take care of other people.

Think of counseling like an oxygen mask on an airplane. Have you ever been on a plane? Before every flight, the flight attendants go through the song and dance about the safety instructions of being on a plane. *These are your seat belts... here are your exit rows... seat backs and tray tables in the upright position... etc.* During this emergency equipment portion of the show, they talk about the face masks dropping from above you. They always tell you that you must first put on your own facemask before attempting to help someone else with theirs.

When I was a kid, I thought that was selfish. *You mean my mom should save herself first before trying to save me?* That thought mildly offended me. I'm sure you have had a similar thought. *Is the 30 seconds it takes to put on a kid's mask next to me really that important?* The simple answer is, "YES." Not to get all science-y on you, but a person can develop hypoxia from a lack of oxygen if the cabin of the plane is depressurized. Hypoxia is a deficiency in the amount of oxygen reaching your brain, tissues and other vital organs, which can lead to a variety of symptoms. Every person is different. Therefore, you do not know how you will react to a lack of oxygen. You could sweat, wheeze, or pass out in a scenario like this. NASA does hypoxia training for astronauts where they must perform menial tasks like sorting toys by shape to show the effects of hypoxia, because one of the most common symptoms is confusion. It would be hard to help a child or other people if you are confused by simple tasks or passed out due to a lack of oxygen. The flight attendants are not performing the facemask song and dance for their health, they are doing it for yours!

Now that I am older, I totally get the rationale behind putting on the oxygen mask first. I will be no help to my 6-year-old son in a situation like this on a plane if I neglect to take care of myself first. First, I secure my mask, and then I can get his in place. After helping him, I may be able to help others, if needed. The same concept can be applied to counseling. I have to take care of myself mentally and physically before I can really help other people. I am unable to truly provide help to others if I neglect myself in the process. You must first take care of yourself before you can ever dream to take care of anyone else. It's worth stating again, it is not selfish to take care of yourself.

In your mind, counseling may be a 4-letter word. Maybe your family frowns upon it. Maybe you believe by going to counseling you are showing weakness. Perhaps you feel that society might look down on you if you admit to having a problem that you can't solve on your own. There are many barriers to counseling. Let's list a few of those barriers here and discuss the realities of them, shall we?

- **Pride**–My entire life I was taught that too much pride was a bad thing. We should be humble, right? We shouldn't brag about who we are or what we have. We shouldn't make people feel as if we are better than them. However, I understand a slightly altered definition of pride now. Yes, we should be humble and not belittle people, but there is more to it than just that. That is a surface level pride. I believe that the real pride we need to fight is being in a place where we are too prideful to ask for help. Because, in our minds, asking for help will show weakness and weakness will mean that someone will have the upper hand on us. I felt that way for a long time. I was miserable inside and hated myself. It was like being trapped in a hole, but being so full of pride I couldn't just reach out my hand to ask someone to pull me out. How stubborn. How sad. Asking for help is not a sign of weakness. It is a sign of strength because a strong person acknowledges their weaknesses and actively tries to overcome those weaknesses. As Dr. Phil would say, "You can't change what you don't acknowledge."[18]

- **Embarrassment**–This kind of goes back to the pride thing because embarrassment is the reason some people hide behind a wall of pride. *What will other* *people think of me?* Here's an answer for you… nothing. Most people wouldn't even bat an eye if they found out you were going to counseling. Besides, people wouldn't even know unless you told them. Seeking treatment through counseling is none of anyone else's business. Remember, this is about you taking care of *you*. This is self-preservation. There is nothing to be embarrassed by about that. In fact, you should take some pleasure in this accomplishment because you saw a weakness and sought help from an expert to overcome that weakness. Why do you think companies pay millions of dollars to motivational coaches to come and speak to their organizations? Because counseling helps to overcome mental barriers, and it helps in all aspects of life, mentally, emotionally, personally and professionally. Look at counseling as coaching. You are seeking help from an expert to help you plan coping mechanisms that will help you jump through the personal hoops in your life. Don't be embarrassed, be empowered.

- **<u>Money</u>**–Money is always an issue no matter who you are, whether you were raised on a porch (like me) or with a silver spoon in your mouth. My first thought about going to counseling was simple. *Who's going to pay for this lavish expense?* There were points that my insurance situation was if-y at best. *Will they pay for something like that? If so, what is my co-pay? Can I find someone that will accept my insurance?* The thought of jumping through these flaming hoops just to go to counseling, which was a concept I wasn't 100% sold on, was overwhelming. Little did I know, there were counseling services on my campus... for free. I had no clue. I never knew about the resources right at my fingertips. I know now I wasn't an exception because most students don't. At the campus where I work, there are three different facilities that offer counseling services to students for little to no cost. It would be worth it for you to find out the money/health insurance/resource situation available to you for counseling services on your campus. Honestly, this might be the last time you get free counseling. Take advantage while you can.

• **Resources**–As I mentioned before, my current campus has at least three different facilities that offer some counseling services to students. You might not have that many at your campus, but I'm willing to bet that there is some sort of resource in the community for you. *How do I find something like that?* As president George W. Bush said back in the day, consult "the Google." All you need to do is type in your institution's name and the word "counseling" and *BOOM*! It's like magic. I'm willing to bet that you will find a site or link to some counseling resources you will find beneficial. If you don't, I will buy you a cup of coffee. Another thing you can do is ask someone on campus like an academic advisor or a success coach. They are trained to know the various resources available to students. If they do not know specifics, they should be able to point you in the right direction. Every place is different and has different resources available. All you have to do is look for them. It is as simple as that.

- **Time**–*Who's got time to be going to counseling sessions every week?* In the words of Sweet Brown, "Ain't nobody got time for that!" (If you don't know who that is, then you got to YouTube the auto-tune remix! The song will stay in your head ALL DAY LONG. And... you're welcome!) Being "too busy" is a myth. My mom would always say there is no such thing as being "too busy." We just chose to not make something a high enough priority. Instead of dismissing not doing something by saying you are "too busy," acknowledge that you didn't place it high enough on your list of priorities. Your mental health is a priority. Deep down, we both know we make time for the things we want to do. You DO have the time to give yourself in the name of self-preservation. One hour a week. What is that? Nothing! A new study reveals that the average person spends 18 minutes trying to decide what they want to stream on Netflix.[19] Let's be generous and say that you only stream videos 3 days a week. *Yeah right! We both know the truth!* That is 54 minutes each week that you waste, my friends. Surely you can use that time more efficiently on yourself. Don't let Netflix win. Make yourself a priority by prioritizing time to take care of yourself by going to a counseling appointment.

So, did counseling solve all of my problems in life? Yes and no. Counseling was not a quick fix for me and it won't be for you either. Counseling gave me the tools to use to overcome challenges when I faced them. Counseling was an investment in my future. Going to counseling helped me come up with coping mechanisms that lead to my success in college and in my career. It helped me so much that I decided to pursue a master's in counseling to help others who face similar problems.

Now that you understand to take care of yourself and how to use the resources to help you overcome life's challenges, you need to find your people. *Who will be my friends on campus? How will I find people that I like? I'm not a tool, but how do I make friends?* If any of these thoughts ran through your mind, then you definitely need to read the last chapter. You need to find out whether it's better to be a tourist or a townie. Which is best? I guess you'll have to find out.

One Page Memo – Counseling

During rough times of transition, adjusting to a new normal can sometimes feel like drowning. There is nothing wrong with going to counseling for help.

Who, What, When, Where, Why and How on Mastering this Memo

- **How?** Google your institution's name and counseling
- **What?** See what comes up for your institution
- **When?** Hours of operation
- **Who?** Contact information (email and phone)
- **Where?** Office location and location of community resources
- **Why?** You don't have to suffer alone. Talking and venting always helps

Sometimes we need a different perspective or to develop new coping mechanisms to get through life's challenges. Find the counseling resources that will help you with the following:

- Depression and/Anxiety Relationships
- Adjustment issues
- Death or other loss
- Alcohol and Drugs identity/issues
- Life goals

-
- Anger
- Past hurts
- Sexual

YOUR MEMO – Counseling

- Where are the counseling services for students on/near campus?

- What is the contact information? Hours of operation?

- What services do they offer?

- How would you make an appointment?

- Is there a waiting list?

- Do you have to fill out an application?

- Is there a fee? If so, how much?

Aurora Alexander

MEMO NOTES

Memo #9

Townie vs. Tourist

"When in Rome, live as the Romans do; when elsewhere, live as they live elsewhere." – Saint Ambrose

My ultimate goal when traveling is to NOT look like a tourist. I know that it sounds bizarre, but it's just something I want to achieve. I want to look as if I live there. I want other people who live in that place to look at me and think I am a local too. To me, it's the ultimate compliment when I travel to a destination, and someone comes up to ask me for directions. I'm not sure why I get such gratification from this, but I'm guessing it is because of the negative connotation associated with being a tourist.

Right now, in the theatre of your mind, picture the

person you think of when you hear the word "tourist." I'll tell you what I think of, and it is not pretty. I think of someone wearing an "I (heart) NY" t-shirt with a goofy hat, socks with sandals, wearing a fanny pack (not a cool Gucci fanny pack) with a giant camera around the neck and a map in their hands. *Yikes!* Now, I know that this is an extreme caricature of what a tourist looks like, but this exaggerated figure has been solidified in my thoughts over many years of travel. I can definitely tell locals, or as I like to call them "townies," from tourists.

I also thought townies looked cool. They have an air of confidence in the most mundane situations. They know where they are going. They always know about the best places to eat and hang out. They also know how to avoid the tourist traps. Townies can tell you the best way to get from A to B without taking the tourist route. Townies are used to taking the back roads and side streets to get where they need to be. You never see them stumbling around with a map in their hands and pointing up to buildings and signs.

If you've never noticed, now you will. Look around at the individuals who live in NYC, Miami, London, Paris... etc. They look different. Each place has its own vibe and the people that dwell within those places, for the most part, carry that same vibe. It's hard to put into words. But when you see it, you know it. When I was in NYC, I felt like the townies were always in a hurry. If I were to just take my time by meandering, I would get mowed over by the traffic of people on the sidewalk. New Yorkers walk with hurried purpose. Tourist meander about like a feather in the wind. Paris, on the other hand, was much more relaxed. The

Parisians that I know believe in *La vie est belle,* and *La belle vie*, which is "Life is beautiful" and "The good life." The people embraced an atmosphere that was carefree, almost tranquil. I came to understand that Parisians and New Yorkers appreciate time in different ways.

Alright, so let's play a little game, shall we? If you had to, who would you rather hang with for an evening, Townie or Tourist? Which person do you think could tell you about the best restaurants (and the worst) in town, Townie or Tourist? Who do you think would know the back roads and the quickest (easiest) way to navigate to and from, Townie or Tourist? Which one of these individuals could tell you the good, the bad and the ugly about the location, Townie or Tourist? You got it... a townie.

Soooo... what's my point? My point is... are you going to be a townie or a tourist on your campus? Are you going to be plugged into what's going on or are you going to sail through school without soaking up any of the happenings on campus or in the town? Both options are very valid realities that are easily attainable. However, one option happens on accident, and other happens by choice. Are you going to blow around campus like a feather in the wind with no direction or are you going to be intentional about your involvement? What you choose or don't choose to be a part of could make all the difference in your college experience. By taking advantage of what is unique to your campus and to your area will help you create a sense of belonging that townies feel. What's the hurt in at least trying it out? The choice is ultimately up to you, but I would put some thought into it now while you have the chance. Which path will you take in your college journey, Townie or Tourist?

Everyone says college is about trying out new things. It's a time to expand your horizons and experiment. You can try out new subjects by taking electives. This is a time when you audition things you think you might like. Maybe you come from a small town where there weren't a lot of opportunities, and now you find yourself at a bigger school where there are tons of prospects. Or maybe you meet someone that introduces you to a new hobby, or you see a flyer on campus for a new club or an upcoming event. In college, you are afforded the luxury of testing out fresh ideas. Before you know it, you will toe the company line at a job and every day will seem just like the one before it. College is one of the few times in life when it is assumed that you will explore new things. But that's not your only job in college.

I would argue that one of the biggest tasks in college is establishing a *new* normal. I'm sure you can remember from the previous memo that I struggled in doing so. I can safely bet that your daily life in college will not be a mind-blowing, frame-of-mind-shifting exploration. There will be opportunities that pop up here and there, but it really comes down to just one thing. In the process of establishing a *new* normal, what will your life look like on campus? Again, assuming you do not have a crystal ball, it is hard to predict. *Or is it?* In a normal week, what does your life look like when you are not in college? Are you in a sport? Are you in any clubs? Do you go to church? Do you volunteer? Do you play an instrument or in a/the band? If you said "yes" to any of those questions, then it is safe to say that you probably have some friends in there. Those people identify with your same interests, values, and passion. Those individuals are *your people*.

Sometimes in life, we make things a bit harder than they need to be. Yes, we should be open to new things, new people and new opportunities. However, we don't have to re-invent the wheel. If you liked *your people* at home before you started college, there is a strong possibility you will find *your people* in a similar environment or doing a similar activity. As high school life fades in the rearview mirror of your mind, sometimes the friendships do too. And that's okay. What is not okay is for you to sit in your room and wonder how to get out there to meet people. Try to establish a routine where you are doing similar things that brought you joy in your old life and incorporate those things into your new life in college. Finding your people is a primitive need when you are establishing your *new* normal in college.

The idea of finding your people and establishing a new normal may sound totally basic. *Of course, I know that I need to make friends... duh! Thanks, Captain Obvious.* But, I would be willing to bet that it has probably been a while since you have made new friends. You might not have been in a scenario where you truly had to swim for yourself since you were like a freshman in high school, possibly even before that. If you have been lucky enough to live in the same place for an extended period of time, you might know everybody that went to your school since you were in kindergarten. At that age, being someone's friend just happens naturally. It was easy to become someone's friend when you were playing with Play-Doh and playing Duck Duck Goose, but when was the last time that happened? You might be a little rusty at making friends at this point. Making friends with new people is like working out a muscle. We all have that muscle inside us, but we haven't had to work it out in a while. So, this muscle becomes soft and flabby. It might take a little time to rebuild that friend-making muscle again by trying to make connections through the activities, hobbies, and environments you found yourself in before. This will help you create a base and strengthen your confidence to where you can venture out to try new things.

● ● ●

Jacob was struggling with his math course the fall semester of his freshman year. Although Jacob was a freshman, he was in his late 20s, and this was his first experience with college. When I saw him during his academic advising appointment, he talked about feeling lost at the university. As a first generation student, Jacob wondered if he was cut out for college and if this path was the right fit for him.

During the appointment, I did my best to narrow down the source of Jacob's frustration. He said he was struggling with classes and feeling connected. Jacob was feeling out of place. I asked Jacob if he had used any of the resources that were on campus to help him feel connected or to help him get through his courses. He said no. I asked him if he knew about tutoring services. He said he knew tutoring was available, but he never went. I asked him if he had heard about the peer mentor program that was offered within his major. He said, "maybe." As we continued to talk, I mentioned other resources on campus that might be of use to Jacob as he continued down his educational path such as Adult Services or the Men's Resource Network.

For the first time during the appointment, Jacob's eyes filled with hope. I could tell that a light bulb was lit above Jacob's head. He suddenly realized that there were resources out there to help him. I stressed to Jacob that he was not alone because these resources were created to help individuals just like him. He could see his collegiate journey through a different lens. His new lease on life reminded me of a similar realization I experienced on my path through college.

• • •

Back in the 80s and early 90s, there was a TV show called *Cheers*.[20] Unless you've heard your parents or grandparents reference the show, I highly doubt you've ever watched it. The characters on that show took their final bow nearly a decade before most of you were even born. However, you may have heard the theme song in passing. Everyone in my generation and older knows the theme song. It would behoove you to type in "Cheers Intro" on YouTube to see what I'm talking about. It's pretty catchy. The song is literally 1 minute. You won't regret listening to it.

The reason I bring up Cheers and the theme song is because of the words and the emotions they provoke. The beginning of the song starts off on a familiar note. It talks about how hard living life can be. The song talks about taking a break from the everyday stresses by just getting away for a while, which makes perfect sense. Then the catchy chorus starts. It talks about going to a place where everyone knows who you are. Those people are always happy that you are there. This a place where you can forget about life for a while. These people are *your* people. These people get you. They get who you are as a person. The reason that the television show and the theme song resonated with people so much is because those are real feelings. Everybody wants to feel a sense of belonging. When life is garbage, and you feel like crap, you want to be surrounded by people who understand. It is the little things in life like somebody just knowing your name, which can turn your day around. This song really tapped into this feeling that everyone, at one time or another, feels.

This song also dances around one of the biggest fears out there, loneliness. Loneliness is awful. And I'm not talking about the concept of being alone. There is a huge difference between being alone and being lonely. Being alone is a fact. If you are alone, you are unaccompanied. You are only. You are solo. Being lonely is totally different because it is a feeling. Being lonely is feeling friendless with even a tinge of hopelessness. Nobody wants to feel lonely, friendless or hopeless. That's why it is important for you to find belonging on campus. Find a place where you know "everybody knows your name," whether it is with a club, organization or job. Over time, you will develop a sense of ownership and pride with this group of people. The feeling of belonging can make all the difference in the world for a successful adjustment to college.

For someone who desperately did not want to look like a tourist in the places I traveled, I find it ironic how I was a tourist at my own school. I was a TOTAL TOURIST! The only thing missing was a horrible fanny pack. *Barf!* I showed up to class, and I left. Next day, I showed up to class, and I left. Next day, I showed up to class, and I left. (Rinse and repeat) I had friends that went to my school, but I only really knew them from work or from my hometown or from friends of friends. None of the individuals I hung out with were in my major, and I very rarely saw them on campus. I didn't willingly spend time on campus, and I didn't intentionally try to get to know anybody in my classes. I was never part of any groups, clubs or organizations on campus. I treated school like an obstacle or a chore I had to power through. For me, spending time on campus was like doing laundry. I only did it if I REALLY had to and even then it was not a certainty. *Do I have to wash these jeans, or can I get one more wear out of them? Do I have to go to class today or can I just sleep in?*

Unlike me, most, if not all, of my friends were involved in other things on campus. I never realized until recently just how vast of a difference there was between my involvement on campus compared to my friends. Looking back, I can see that the difference was significant. I had friends that were involved with Greek life through various sororities and fraternities. There was always something scheduled like a volunteer opportunity, a fund-raising event or a party that my friends were attending on campus. Some of my friends were involved in a team sport like baseball, cheerleading or an intramural league. Again, these individuals had organized events throughout the semester on top of practices and games they had to attend. I had a couple of friends that held positions within some student clubs and organizations on campus. Those students were always on campus to promote events or have meetings with the executive board to keep the group afloat. The rest of my friends had on-campus jobs that plugged them into the school. One friend worked as a guide for orientation. She had a blast. She got to learn so much about what the school offered by attending the trainings. Plus, she met a ton of new people every semester. All of my friends were really plugged into the college and the campus. Me? Not so much.

When I walked across the stage for graduation, I was definitely not a townie. I just oozed tourist-y vibes. I was not plugged into my campus, my major or my department. Nothing! Except for the six tickets they allotted me for my graduation day, which were all used by my family, I didn't know another soul at my graduation ceremony. In a sea of caps and gowns, I didn't know another graduate. After all the time I spent trying to get through school, it's hard to imagine that I knew no one there that day. No fellow students, no familiar faces from the faculty. Nada! To be honest, it felt odd. Now that I work in higher education, I see that it's more common than you would probably think. Again, being a tourist on campus can happen by accident. Being a townie is intentional.

Luckily, I had another chance at getting plugged in and becoming a townie when I was getting my master's. I knew everyone in my department, and everyone knew me. I didn't look at going to class or being on campus as a chore. In fact, I looked forward to the opportunities of being on campus. Because of my involvement, I was chosen to serve as the student representative for the Counseling and Human

Development committee, which was a big honor. I was also chosen out of everyone in the program to do a short advertising video to talk about the program. That little video is still on the school's website to this day. There was no doubt that I was a townie. I was an intentional student who was invested in my education, my degree program and my campus, which differed totally from my previous college experience.

What I think we fail to realize when we are in college is that our need to be part of something in order to satisfy that sense of belonging is ingrained within us at a very early age. We played games and formed clubs based on fulfilling this need. This necessity for inclusion is something we actively seek when we are children. I'll give you an easy example.

Did you ever play freeze tag as a kid? There were always alternative games of tag, but freeze tag was my ultimate favorite. Freeze tag was awesome because it was a classic game. There was no set-up needed, no equipment required, you could play it anywhere, and it didn't matter how many people were playing. We could have 3 kids or 30 kids. It truly didn't matter. We always had fun, and we did it all without spending a dime. *When was the last time that happened?*

There were only three important rules to remember for freeze tag.

1. If the person who is "it" tags you, you have to "freeze" in place like a statue.
2. The only way to get unfrozen is if someone else untagged you.

3. "Base" was a designated safe area where you could not be tagged.

Rules 2 and 3 are crucial. It may not seem like it on the surface, but they are rules to live by.

First, establish a "base." Even as a 5-year-old, I knew I needed to get to the base. Kids instinctively know they need to have access to some kind of home base to be safe. Unfortunately, we kind of forget about that as we get older. More and more things climb the priority lists that we make for ourselves, and we forget about the basics. Our "base" is our default. We know that when life gets real, return to base. When things get tough and we need to regroup, return to base. That has always been the standard in life, you just didn't realize it.

As kids, we even know that we need other people to help "unfreeze" us from time to time. It's no different as a college student. Sometimes you need to be "unfrozen" or find refuge at your "home base" just like in freeze tag. Create a base on campus and form a team with those people. These people can help "unfreeze" you when you need it. The home base will provide you with a place to go on campus that will help you get refueled before heading out into the game again.

Let's see how far I can stretch this analogy, shall we? Maybe classic freeze tag is not your jazz. There are other slightly altered versions of the classic game out there like, flashlight tag, animal freeze tag or cartoon freeze tag. That's cool. *Whatever.* You can choose your own adventure. Find the people, the game, and/or the group you click with the most. That's one of the best things about college, finding out who you are and figuring out the answers to "Where is my base?" And "Who can unfreeze me when I need help?"

This analogy spoke volumes about my experience when I was getting my bachelor's and master's degrees. During my bachelor's degree, I had no home base. There was no "base" for me on campus where I could just relax or get recharged. The whole experience of college was draining to me. Because I had no "base," I didn't feel that I had anyone to help "unfreeze" me when I needed it.

On the other hand, my freeze tag game during my graduate program was on Fleek! Being on campus and hanging out in my department felt like a second home. I knew there were people to talk to, and I knew where to find them. There were many, many times I needed help. I knew where to find people to "unfreeze" me out of the tough spot. My grades were better, and I enjoyed the entire experience. This time when I graduated with my master's, I knew everyone that was graduating with my degree. I was part of a group and I no longer felt isolated. I am still close with many of those people to this day. I can see now it was well worth my time to invest in finding *my* people.

You may have heard this phrase expressed as simple as "When in Rome..." The meaning behind the expression is self-explanatory. When a person is visiting a place foreign to them, they should follow the customs of those who live in it. As much pride as I had for "living as the Romans do" when I traveled, I completely failed the "When in Rome..." concept when it came to my own college experience. Okay, so going to college may not be as much of a culture shock as traveling abroad, but don't dismiss the gravity of the cultural shift in college. College, as an incoming freshman, is foreign territory. Even if you were lucky enough to take college courses while in high school, it still doesn't completely prepare you for what's to come.

In high school, there's a building, there's a place, there's an office where you know you can go to find answers. College is so big, even on the smaller campuses, it's hard to know where to look. There are so many buildings, wings, and offices. There is no *one* place on a college campus. It's hard to be grounded if there is not "a place." Not all of your classes will be in the same building that your major's main office is housed. It's challenging to find your bearings in a new environment like this. However, finding a group, club, organization or experience on campus can help you feel grounded while providing you with the foundational base needed.

Again, find *your* people and create a base by making connections on campus. Avoid being a tourist by following the simple list below.

- **<u>Join</u>**–Anything that interests you! Whether it is a club, Greek life or volunteering, be part of something to feel a sense of belonging.

- **<u>Attend Class</u>**–ALWAYS! Do not treat going to class like it is a chore. When you miss a class, you miss out. Even though you are an adult because you technically don't *have* to go to class, you are still missing out on information and connections that will help you out later on down the road.

- **<u>Don't Be Afraid</u>**–To be yourself, try to new things or to take a chance.

One Page Memo – Townie vs. Tourist

Get plugged-in to your campus by finding *your people* and creating a home base. Make friends and don't reinvent the wheel.

Who, What, When, Where, Why and How on Mastering this Memo

- **What?** Find *your people*
- **How?** Look, ask and be open to involvement
- **When?** Meeting times and calendar of events
- **Who?** Contact information (email and phone)
- **Where?** Anywhere on campus!
- **Why?** Sometimes you need people to "unfreeze" you during tough times

"You wanna be where you can see, our troubles are all the same. You wanna be where everybody knows your name."

Find your people by joining and/or participating in the following:

- Social/Academic/Religious club
- Student Government
- Become a tutor
- Attend campus events
- Community Service and Volunteering
- Greek Life
- School Paper
- Intramural sports
- On-campus job

YOUR MEMO – Townie vs. Tourist

- What were your "bases" in high school?

- Are there similar clubs/groups/activities on campus?

- What is the name of the office that organizes clubs on campus?

- What are some new clubs/groups/activities that look interesting?

- Do they have any upcoming events?

- What is the contact information?

Aurora Alexander

MEMO NOTES

EPILOGUE

You don't belong here. I was petrified that at any moment, somone would look at me in class and call me out. If I said the wrong answer or asked a dumb question, I knew there was a chance that I would blow my cover. *You're not smart enough.* As I got older, my fears began to fester and grow into something more sinister. *You're too old.* I felt like the odd person out in every class. All of those previous fears flourished over time because it was nurtured in the rich, fertile ground of self-loathing, guilt and shame. *You're not good enough.*

I didn't initially have these fears when I first started college. However, as I struggled and meandered through, these fears began to take root in my mind. Growing and growing and growing, they took on a life of their own. Even when I did excel in an assignment, on a test or a class, I felt that all of my other failures overshadowed any good that I achieved. I was so defeated. I was virtually paralyzed. With all of the time that I had spent in college, I only had 3 semesters left. Unfortunately, I felt like I had no momentum or motivation to move forward. The light at the end of the tunnel was still too dim.

Then fate happened. In the middle of all of my misery and confusion, I became pregnant. *Me? Pregnant?* The weight of reality hit me like a ton of bricks. I began to brainstorm of how I would legitmately take care of a baby. I wondered what kind of job would allow me to have a life where I could see my kid or be with my baby when needed? I went back to the familiar well. Nurse? *NO! Of course not!* Coal miner? *Get real!* I was panicked about my future and the future of my baby.

I actually had a great job working as a Business Development Manager for a team of car dealerships in Kentucky. However, I knew that my line of work was demanding. Weekends and holidays were shot because those are big car selling days! I would be expected to be at work. I'd be missing out on time with my baby. I had to do a shift in my career. I felt that my only choice was to go back to college.

Holding my son in my arms for the first time was life-changing. Looking down at his sweet little face altered my universe. His innocent eyes looking up at mine lit a fire inside of me that I can't quite explain. I knew that his life was totally dependent upon me. I couldn't cower in the corner anymore like a sore-tailed cat after a fight with a dog. I had to pull myself up by my bootstraps and start moving forward for the sake of my son, Fox. And that's just what I did.

My son was born in October and I was back in school by January. I knew that I needed to finish what I had started so long ago. I had faith that finding a career would just *come to me* as I reached the finish line. Luckily, it did, but it wasn't an accident. I had many in-depth converations with *myself* to figure out my interests. I methodically compared them to particular careers. Then I made an honest pros and cons list. The pros and cons list had knocked me out of the study abroad program many years before, but I was determined to make this list work in my favor to help me make a choice.

I had finally narrowed down that I wanted to be a counselor, a school counselor. I did have a caring nature and I enjoyed listening to people's problems. I could see myself exceling in an environment where I provided individuals with guidance on how to overcome obstacles much like I needed in school. I thought school counseling would be nice because I could have access to my son, if needed. I would have the same days off, holidays and summers as Fox. *This sounds like a no-brainer!*

In my research, I found that I needed to go to graduate school in order to obtain the license necessary to work as a school counselor. I had worked so hard to pull up my grades from a 1.8 GPA. I was now poised to graduate with a 3.25 GPA. I was eligible to apply to most counseling programs as long as I had a 3.0 GPA or above and I made the cut. *Holla!* In the earlier chapters, you heard about my disaster of a graduate school interview and how I was wildly unprepared to answer any of the questions. Fortunately for me, I was chosen to be part of the newest cohort that started in fall.

At this point, I was actually really proud of myself. I didn't graduate with honors or with a special sash, but I graduated. I never thought that day would come. I looked up at my family as I walked across the stage, but I could barely see them because of the tears that were welled up in my eyes. I was a naive hillbilly girl from a little pissant country town in podunk West Virginia. If I had never graduated from high school, I'm not sure anyone would have been too shocked. The expecations of me making something of myself were low except from my mom. On that day, I made my mom proud and I surprised myself. There was a peace in my heart. I had accomplished my goal and I was ready to take on my next adventure, a master's degree.

Even though I was accepted into a master's program because I had met the requirements, I still felt... *off*. It's hard to describe. I felt that everyone else in my cohort were the same, but somehow I was different. Even though we all made it into the same program, had similar grades, varying ages and backgrounds, I felt that I was set apart from the rest. Nobody *made* me feel different. I just felt that I was different from everyone else. Even though I made friends in the program, I still felt alone. No matter how well I did in my classes, I couldn't quite shake this feeling. I felt this feeling before in my bachelor's program, but nothing as severe as this. Each passing semester, this feeling would gain intensity inside of me.

On the outside, I was a high-achieving student. On the inside, however, I felt inferior to everyone else in my cohort. Every semester, I feared that I would finally face the class that would bring me to my knees. *Will this be the class that knocks me out of the program? Will this class be the hurdle that I just can't clear?* As happy as I was to finish another semester, check off another few classes in my program, take a few more steps toward graduation, I was quickly brought back down to earth with my crippling fear of failing.

The first 4-6 weeks of a class was like torture until I received my first grade or two in the course. Again, at this point, I knew that grades were just a reflection of my absorption of the material. I didn't want an A for the sake of receiving an A. I wanted to *earn* an A. However, I was consumed with the absorption aspect now. *What if my brain can't absorb anymore material?* I know that may sound ridiculous and it even seems ridiculous typing it out, but it was no less of a fear for me. I would do the assigned readings. I would participate in the discussions in class. I would do all that I was supposed to do, but what if it really wasn't sinking in my brain? *Would I be able to recall this information on an exam? Would I be able to eloquently compare the theories to each other in a paper?* Most importantly... *Would I be able to accurately apply these theories in practice when working with people who need genuine help?* The fear festered in my brain.

The feeling wouldn't cease until after the first big paper or test. Once I received a good grade, an A, then I would allow myself to take a breath of relief. *My secret is safe. No one will catch on that I'm an incompetent failure... for now.* I saw grades as validation. That validation allowed me to be in the program. The grades, even though they were good, fed into my insecurities. It was a viscious cycle that played out over and over again.

Even my friends noticed the irrational fear. My friend, Clay, would be puzzled by my reaction to an upcoming exam. Everyone would be slightly on edge because of an exam, but I was an extreme case. He would always tell me that I would do well and to just believe in myself, but the fear was palpable. The anxiety would not release its hold on me until I received that grade. Sometimes it would take weeks before I found out how I performed on the exam or paper. I was consumed with my grades. I would even check 10-15 times a day for an update online in the hopes that the instructor posted the grades. This obsession was all stemmed from an overwhelming fear of being found out by my peers and faculty.

I didn't realize it, but this fear had multiplied exponentially in my master's program. To be honest, I kind of knew that it was always there in my bachelor's program. It was in the undercurrent of all of my failures as I bumbled around aimlessly for fouteen years, but this had overtaken my life. Even though I had met the prerequisite requirements for the program, passed the interview process, was voted on by a panel of faculty to get accepted into the program, I was still afraid of everyone finding out my dirty little secret. My fear was not *if*, but *when*. *How long will I be able to keep up this charade? When will they find out that I'm a giant failure hiding behind a string of hollow accomplishments and dumb luck?*

Three semesters into my program and I still felt like a fraud. I had made straight A's and I had a 4.0 GPA for the first time since high school. I was proud, but I still felt like it was a fluke. I had switched tracks during my counseling program where my focus was on student affairs in higher education because I wanted to help students like me. I started delving deep into the world of higher education, but I still carried that sense of impending doom. It wasn't until I attended a conference session for student affairs professionals that I was able to put a name to my fear. My irrational fear was called imposter syndrome. Imposter syndrome is an extreme pattern of thoughts where an individual doubts their own achievements while nursing an incessant feeling of dread for the potential of being exposed as a fake or a charlatan.

What? This is a <u>thing</u>? I couldn't believe my ears. It was everything that I could do to not run out of the conference session crying. I sat in my chair totally frozen. I felt like I had a huge spotlight on me. I felt like a little girl who's crush found her diary. It was like the presenter was telling everyone my deepest, darkest secrets. My cheeks were flushed with humiliation. I had been exposed. In that moment, I was afraid of drawing too much attention to myself. I knew that if I would have shifted in my chair or rustled some papers or made a dramatic exit, everyone would realize who I really was... a nobody. Someone that was not worthy of an education, not smart enough to do better and not good enough to achieve more.

That realization was difficult to process at first. The term "imposter syndrome" floated through my mind relentlessly for the next few weeks. However, once it sank in, I realized that I wasn't *crazy*. I also realized that I wasn't alone. There were others that felt my pain and my panic. Even though that pill was hard to swallow, sometimes you need a pill to feel better. This was the medicine that I needed to step outside of my false perception in order to have a clear view of the truth. I needed that dose of reality to shoot holes in my incompentent failure narrative that I had constructed in my brain. My achievements were *real* accomplishments. There was no trickery or slight of hand involved in getting into my master's program. *I did it*! I was not pulling the wool over anyone's eyes when it came to my good grades. I *earned* those A's. *That was all me!*

This feeling of being a fraud had been growing inside of

me since I was a little girl and I didn't even realize it. I never really needed to try to make A's in school. I always received high marks and gold stars. I was a "natural" at most things, which sounds pretty amazing when you look at it from a distance. However, someone who is a natural in a lot of areas will fail to create coping mechanisms for overcoming obsticles. Whenever I faced an obsticle or a hurdle in life, I dodged it. If I didn't immediately master what I was doing, I avoided it like the plague. This means that I side-stepped real challenges in life. This strategy did not adequately prepare me for the future.

As an adult, I faced challenges, almost daily, that I didn't immediately master. If I had the slightest setback, my confidence would crash. Instead of looking at the mistake, making mental notes about what went wrong and moving forward, I would completely evade the issue. I would just bury my head in the sand and pretend like it didn't exist, which only made my problems worse. This was a horrible pattern that I created in life. However, I finally understood where this came from and how to overcome this pattern.

Moving forward, I still struggled with those feelings of inferiority, but those feelings no longer controlled my actions. I just kept pushing forward to achieve my goals. I ended up graduating from my master's program with a 3.98 GPA. I ended up getting a job at the institution where I always wanted to work, Kent State University. I was really proud of myself for accomplishing my goals. I had far exceeded any expectations that my mom had for me. *I did it! I finally did it!*

Unfortunately, that feeling of *something must be wrong*

with me never fully went away. I know that I had accomplished my goal of graduating college and graduating with a master's, but I still focused on my struggle. *Why did it take me so long? Why was I the only one that didn't know how to succeed in college? How did I not know, but everyone else did? What memos did I miss?*

When I started working as an academic advisor there were so many things to learn. It was quite overwhelming. Over time I got the hang of the substitutions, exceptions and curriculum jargon. The one thing that I truly loved about my job was my interactions with the students, but I noticed a common theme with each one. A pattern was forming that I didn't think was possible. I noticed that a majority of my students were completely clueless to how college works. They came in with questions and I had answers. These questions weren't bizarre or out of left field. These were the same exact questions that I had when I was in college. *Wait?!? I'm not the only one?!? Other people struggle in college?*

After the first year of working as an academic advisor, after answering the same questions over and over and over, I had a major realization. *People are not inherently born with the knowledge of how to succeed in college!* What someone should do or how they should do it is not genetically hardwired into a person's DNA. We learn so many things in high school, but we are never taught these specific things. My dad used to say to me when I was a little girl, "Tying your shoes is simple. But if you don't know how to tie your shoes, it's simply awful." Students don't know what they don't know. *I wasn't an incompetent fool. I simply didn't know.*

I answer the same questions for students every day.

These are the same exact questions that I had while I was milling around in my bachelor's. Most students seem embarrassed, maybe even a little ashamed, for asking these questions. My reaction is always the same. *Don't be embarrassed to ask. How else would you know? Did you read a book about it? Did they teach you this in a class? Were you tested on this? Of course not.* Students may be prepped for some of the subjects that they will learn in college, but no one ever warns them about this. No one teaches this stuff! The average student doesn't know how to successfully navigate college. How can we expect for students to know if no one has shown them the path?

So that, my friends, is why I decided to write this book. I can only meet with a fixed number of students each semester. I can't reach all college students in my current position. However, I knew that if I wrote a book and openly talked about my experiences, failures and mistakes, I could potentially help more students. If I can reach more students to teach more students, maybe I can save a few from floundering like I did. Now, that is my professional mission in life. Ultimately, I want students to get the memos that I missed.

Thanks for reading! Please add a short review on Amazon and let me know what you thought! Also go to my website, auroraalexander.com, for my One-Page Memos, as well as other goodies, that will serve as quick-start guides to implementing the tools in this book for free.

ACKNOWLEDGEMENTS

Below is a list of people that I would like to acknowledge for helping with the creation of this book. No matter how big or how little of a part you played, I want to say thank you from the bottom of my heart. With your help, I've been able to accomplish a dream of mine that I've had for more than 20 years. You'll never know how appreciative I am for your contribution.

This list is in no particular order:

- **My son, Fox**

  If it weren't for you, I would still be floating around life like a feather in the wind. You gave me a direction and you gave me purpose. You will never know who I was before you were born and I'm so thankful for that. I love you more than *everything*.

- **Mom**

  You are my best friend. I'm so thankful for what you've taught me in life. I know that I am truly loved. My greatest fear in life was disappointing you even though you tell me every day how proud you are of me. I hope you know how proud I am of you. You are my #1 fan and I am yours. Thank you for your love and support. I love you forever.

- **My family**

  You have put up with my shenanigans for years. You loved me even though I was completely unsure of myself and incapable of making a thoughtful decision. Even though my life has been a series of one step forward and three steps back, you have loved me and supported me anyways. I don't know what I would do without you. I love you and thank you.

- **Dr. Henrique Alvim**

  For two years you were my faculty advisor and my professional mentor. Now, I am pleased to call you my friend and colleague. I have a tremendous amount of respect for you. Even though I had no idea what I was doing and asked a lot of obvious questions, you never once made me feel inferior. I look back and still don't see how you were so patient and wise. I'm thankful for your tutelage. You were able to smooth out my rough edges and turn me into the professional I am today. Thank you.

- **Kent State University**

  I'm thankful that I work for a university that puts an emphasis on academic advising. I'm thankful for my job and I'm thankful for my position here. Kent State has provided me with a professional environment that allows me to continue to grow within my field. The university has also allowed me to provide a good life for myself and my son. When people ask me where I work, I say with pride, "Kent State University!" Thank you.

- **Dr. Maria Zaragoza**

  Thank you for taking a chance on me. I really wanted to work for your department and you made that happen. Every day, I love my job. I have a tremendous amount of respect for who you are as a professional and as a person. I don't know how you do what you do. You juggle so many things, but you always have time to talk to me when I need it. I appreciate you more than you may realize. Thank you.

- **Dr. Clarissa Thompson**

  I know that you are new to the role of Undergraduate Curriculum Coordinator, but I appreciate you none-the-less. You are always open to feedback and new ways to better serve our students. Thank you.

- **Staff and Faculty of the Department of Psychological Sciences**

  Thank you for all of your hard work, your time and your commitment. It is a privilege to work alongside of you. Thank you.

- **Dean Blank, Matthew Minichillo and Mandy Anderson**

  Thank you for recognizing the importance of academic advising and for making it a priority. I appreciate the work that you do and value our good relationship within the college. Your contributions to the college do not go unnoticed. Thank you.

- **Charlie Nutt, PhD, NACADA and KASADA**

  Thank you for all that you do for the profession. The pride that you take in creating opportunities for professional development resonates within the academic advising community. Thank you.

- **Victoria Gutbrod**

  I appreciate all of the help that you have given me over the years. You helped me see through my emotional and mental fog that clouded my way for most of my adult life. Thanks to you I have been able to formulate a future. You had faith in me way before I ever did. Thank you.

-

- **Dana Lawless-Andric**

  You've been such an inspiration to me. Listening to your personal story provided me with validation of my own story. For many years, I was embarrassed of bumbling around school. Talking with you, however, I realized that my college experience can be harnessed to help and inspire other students. You showed me how to embrace my past rather than be ashamed of it. Thank you.

- **Gail Tankersley and Rita Spears**

  I never really understood the purpose of an academic advisor before I met you. I trusted your advice and your insight to get me through school. You told me what I needed to hear when I needed to hear it. You kept me on course and encouraged me as I made my way towards graduation. Our conversations were succinct, yet profound. Thank you.

- **Nancy White and Jessica Wood**

  I am so grateful for everything that you taught me. The things that I learned in your office shaped who I am as a professional and solidified my career path. I admire you both for what you do and who you are. I know that I shed some tears in that office trying to figure out who I was as a person and a professional. I appreciate the time that you invested in me through your guidance and mentorship. Thank you.

- **Kristina Kamis and Rachel Caraffi**

  I appreciate the time you took to read my book. Sometimes I just need another set of eyes and a different perspective. I'm grateful for the feedback that you provided me. Even though you didn't have a horse in this race you still took the time to give me your thoughts. Thank you.

- **Bryce Cain**

  Thank you for all of your encouragement. From day one, you have encouraged me to branch out to explore different avenues within my career field. You've been a sounding board for many of my ideas and ventures. You are the eternal advocate. I admire the passion that you bring to the profession and I value you as a teammate. Thank you for fighting for me, then and now.

- **Krista**

  You are more than a best friend. You are my sister. You were the person I called when I found out that I was having a sister and not a cat! Over the years, I have shown you the lowest of my lows. You have never once flinched, ran away or judged me no matter how absurd my life choices have been. You were the first person to show me what a real friend looks like. I love you, dude. Thank you for putting up with me.

- **Clay Cooper**

  I don't know how many times you have given me sound advice and I have immediately rolled my eyes. *Countless.* As a matter of fact, I'm actually rolling my eyes as I write this. I am grateful to have found a friend that tells me the things I don't want to hear, refuse to hear and choose not to hear. No matter how hard my eyes roll, you never waver. Believe it or not, I appreciate that. From one know-it-all to another, thank you for being my friend.

-

-

- **Jillian Shephard**

  God knows what I need when I need it. That's why you came along in my life when you did. You've been my spiritual mentor, my cheerleader, my coach, my sister and my best friend. No matter how awful my story, you had already faced something similar in your past. You've never judged me even though all I do is judge myself. Your friendship means the world to me. Thank you for being you and choosing to be my friend.

- **Students – Yes, YOU!**

  If it weren't for the students that I encountered my first year as an academic advisor then I wouldn't have seen a need to write this book. I would have continued to believe that there was something wrong with me because I didn't inherently know how to successfully navigate college. Your questions were the inspiration for this book. Without you, I wouldn't love my job. Thank you.

- Last but not least, **Dr. Joel Hughes**

  I can honestly say that if it wasn't for you, this book would not exist. You tirelessly relit the flames of inspiration throughout this process. You have been my editor, proofreader, paginator, contributor, taskmaster, time-keeper, accountability partner, delegator and advisor. I appreciate the sage advice you have given me with this book and in my life. I can never thank you enough for the amount of time you have invested in this project and in me. Through all my doubts, setbacks, second guesses and tears, you helped me accomplish this goal and realize a dream. With all of my heart... Thank you! Thank you! Thank you!

DEDICATION

Dear Younger Me,

It's not your fault. How were you to know? No one ever told you or showed you the way. Your parents didn't know, and their parents didn't know. You must go it alone. You are a stranger in a strange land. And it's okay.

You will never read it in a book or learn it in a class. It will never be the thesis of a paper or on an exam. Try not to beat yourself up too bad though. Oh... who am I kidding? I know that you will torture yourself with guilt because of the "shoulds" and "oughts."

Just know that there is a reason for it all. All your mistakes, missteps, misjudgments and missed memos will lead you to what you have always wanted. One day you will have a son that will be your reason for living. You'll look back someday (like I'm doing now) and know that you would face all those failures again, on the day that you failed, just to have him.

Now pull yourself together, for Fox sake, and go brush your teeth. And start flossing. You'll thank me later.

With all my love and all for Fox,

The Older (and much cooler version) Me

ABOUT THE AUTHOR

Aurora Alexander is an academic advisor at Kent State University and a certified career coach. Desperately unprepared when she first entered college, Aurora made many mistakes on her journey through her undergraduate degree. She aimlessly meandered for fourteen years while pursuing her bachelor's. She clearly missed the memo. Eventually, she prevailed, learning from her mistakes while turning negatives into positives on her path through higher education. Aurora wants all students to be successful and avoid the pitfalls as they navigate their educational adventures. Ultimately, she wants students to get the memos that she missed.

www.auroraalexander.com

REFERENCES

1 *Menken, Alan. "Walt Disney Pictures Presents The Little Mermaid." Milwaukee, WI :H. Leonard Pub. Corp., 1990.*

2 *Shaheen, Jack G. "The Documentary of Art:"The Undersea World of Jacques Cousteau"." The Journal of Popular Culture 21, no. 1 (1987): 93-101.*

3 Cowperthwaite, Gabriela, Manuel V. Oteyza, Eli Despres, Jonathan Ingalls, Chris Towey, and Jeff Beal. 2013. Blackfish.

4 https://www.studentresearchfoundation.org/wp-content/uploads/2018/01/SRF_2018_SOTU.pdf

5 *CBS Home Entertainment ; The Mark Gordon Company ; CBS Television Studios ; ABC Studios. Criminal Minds. The Sixth Season. Hollywood, Calif. :CBS DVD : Paramount, 2011.*

6 *Metro-Goldwyn-Mayer Pictures presents a Marc Platt production ; produced by Marc Platt, Ric Kidney ; screenplay by Karen McCullah Lutz & Kirsten Smith ; directed by Robert Luketic. Legally Blonde. [Santa Monica, CA] :MGM Home Entertainment, 2006.*

7 *Law and Order: Special Victims Unit.* Created by Dick Wolf. National Broadcasting Corporation, 1999 – 2019.

8 Holme, S. A., J. Evans, C. Roberts, and D. L. Roberts. "Everybody's free (to wear sunscreen): the power of pop." *British Journal of Dermatology* 1[4]4, no. 4 (2001): 918-918.

9 https://www.bbc.co.uk/newsround/27130467

10 Wessler, Charles B., Brad Krevoy, Steven Stabler, Peter Farrelly, Bennett Yellin, Bobby Farrelly, Jim Carrey, Jeff Daniels, Lauren Holly, and Karen Duffy. 2005. *Dumb and dumber*. [United States]: Alliance Atlantis.

11 Tolkien, John Ronald Reuel. *The Lord of the Rings: One Volume*. Houghton Mifflin Harcourt, 2012.

12 https://www.westgateresorts.com/blog/i-havent-been-everywhere-but-its-on-my-list/

13 LM, FM, *Point Break*. Directed by Kathryn Bigelow. Hollywood, CA: 20th Century Fox, 1991.

14 Doyle, Arthur Conan. *The Complete Sherlock Holmes*. Vol. 1. Doubleday Books, 1930.

15 Ramsey, Dave. *The Total Money Makeover: Classic Edition: A Proven Plan for Financial Fitness*. Thomas Nelson, 2013.

16 Turner, Bonnie and Turner, Tyler. Tommy Boy. Film. Directed by Peter Segal. USA: Paramount Pictures. 1995

17 Robbins, Tom. *Fierce invalids home from hot climates*. Bantam, 2001.

18 https://www.drphil.com/advice/dr-phils-ten-life-laws/

19 https://www.thewrap.com/netflix-users-browse-for-programming-twice-as-long-as-cable-viewers-study-says/

20 Andrews, Bart, and Cheryl Blythe. *Cheers: the official scrapbook*. New American Library, 1987.

www.ingramcontent.com/pod-product-compliance
Lightning Source LLC
Chambersburg PA
CBHW071531040426
42452CB00008B/977